ONE IN A SERIES FROM THE PUBLISHERS OF *PRE-K TODAY*

LEARNING THROUGH PLAY

DRAMATIC PLAY

A Practical Guide for Teaching Young Children

Edited by Nancy Jo Hereford *and* Jane Schall

Foreword by Sara Smilansky

Contributing Writers:

Ellen Booth Church

Edgar Klugman, Ed.D., and Hertha Klugman

Merle Karnes

Karen Miller

Kathie Spitzley

Sandra Waite-Stupiansky, Ph.D.

Illustrations by Nicole Rubel

Early Childhood Division Vice President and Publisher
Helen Benham

Art Director
Sharon Singer

Production Editor
Katie Corcoran

Consultants
Adele Brodkin Ph.D., Jackie Carter, Susan Kleinsinger

Published by:
Scholastic Inc.
Early Childhood Division
730 Broadway
New York, NY 10003

ISBN # 49112-1
Library of Congress Catalog Number

CONTENTS

LEARNING
AND
GROWING
WITH DRAMATIC PLAY

ACTIVITY
PLANS
FOR TWOS, THREES, FOURS, AND FIVES

COVER PHOTO: © ERIKA STONE 1987

NEVER NEVER LAND

I know a place where dreams are born,
And time is never planned.
It's not on any chart,
You must find it with your heart
Never Never Land.

It might be miles beyond the moon,
Or right there where you stand.
Just have an open mind,
And then suddenly you'll find
Never Never land.

You'll have a treasure if you stay there,
More precious far than gold.
For once you have found your way there,
You can never, never grow old.

So come with me where dreams are born,
And time is never planned.
Just think of lovely things,
And your heart will fly on wings,
Forever, in Never Never Land.

FOREWORD
A CONVERSATION WITH SARA SMILANSKY ABOUT THE VALUE OF DRAMATIC PLAY

Q: What is dramatic play?

A: In dramatic play, children take on the roles of adults who are meaningful in their lives — mommies, daddies, doctors, storekeepers, etc. If a child plays a make-believe role alone, he or she is engaging in dramatic play. It becomes sociodramatic play when the child interacts with another person — child or adult — who is also in a pretend role.

Q: Do children of all ages engage in dramatic play?

A: Children begin taking on roles at about age one and a half. However, children at different levels of development play in different ways. Very young children play alone and are very influenced by the props available. A child may see a doll and begin rocking it, but if that doll was not in sight, he might not think of taking on that nurturing role. By ages four and five, most children are much more adept at socio-dramatic play. They decide on themes, look for props to enhance those themes, assign roles, and develop quite involved play scenarios.

Q: Why is dramatic play important?

A: When you develop a child's skill at dramatic play, that child's development will be enhanced in many other areas as well. This has been demonstrated over and over again in studies done in England, Israel, and the United States.

Q: What areas of development are enhanced through dramatic play?

A: Every area! Take social skills, for example. When a child is skilled at taking on roles, at devising props, and at creating pretend scenarios, he plays well in a group. He is also viewed as a more desirable playmate by others. This ability helps to make the child fun to play with and socially accepted.

Dramatic play also helps young children develop empathy with others, an essential step in moral development. When children take on roles, they mimic the actions and emotions of others. In a rudimentary way, they experience seeing a situation from another point of view.

Dramatic play is also an important avenue for emotional development. Children often use dramatic play as a way to work through fears and confusion. They may act out a frightening scenario about monsters or hurricanes, but they provide themselves with the power to vanquish the monster or to start and stop the howling wind.

Q: How does dramatic play contribute to cognitive development?

A: It develops many areas such as creative thinking and problem-solving skills, but as an example, let's look at how it enhances language development. During dramatic play, children use oral language to communicate their ideas about themes, roles, and props to others and to themselves. When they play doctor, store, or airport, there's a rich opportunity to learn the vocabulary associated with each theme. The more children engage in dramatic play, the better their language skills become. And the better their language skills, the more satisfying their dramatic play.

I also want to stress that the ability to pretend that's developed through dramatic play will help children greatly in all areas of schooling as they grow. Consider what's involved in solving a math problem. The child has to make believe there is a father who gave his son ten oranges, and then this boy's brother took five of those oranges away. The child has to be able to visualize the problem before it will make any sense to him. If children are experienced in make-believe play, they are more capable of creating a mental picture of a situation. That ability also helps them visualize historical events, places on a map, characters in a book, etc.

Q: **What is the adult's role in dramatic play?**

A: The teacher or family member must support dramatic play and recognize the value of this activity. It's true that pretend play is fun for children. We know that it's also vital for social, emotional, and intellectual development.

Adults also need to observe children's dramatic play. Why is it that adults often find time to sit with a child to see how well he is learning pre-reading or math concepts or whether he can write his name, but can't find the time to observe the level at which the child is playing? It goes back to understanding the value of dramatic play.

Q: **What can adults learn by observing dramatic play?**

A: Along with finding out what children like to play and what roles they like to take, an adult can find out whether a child is skilled at dramatic play. There's a tendency to expect that all you have to do is put out toys and children will develop dramatic-play skills. We know that it doesn't happen that simply. Children who are good at taking on roles and pretending have usually had someone in their life — parent, grandparent, sibling, neighborhood playmate — who has engaged in make-believe play with the child. These "models" have also shown by example how to take on roles, and communicated the joy of pretend play. Children who are not good at taking on roles and interacting with others in pretend situations may need help developing higher-level play skills.

Q: **How does an adult help enrich children's dramatic play?**

A: We've found that it's relatively easy to draw children into more complex play. Sometimes all the adult needs to do is introduce a new prop or ask an open-ended question that will get the child thinking. Or the adult might take on a role herself and interact with the child as a way to extend the play. Naturally, the adult does not take over play but follows the child's lead. The adult steps in and out of play, finding ways to enhance and enrich the activity without encroaching on the child's ideas or creativity.

Q: **How would you summarize the value of dramatic play?**

A: People have this notion that play is just some restful activity — something good for the "soul" of a child — or just social in its benefits. It is those things, but we know that it's so much more. Playing pretend is not only good for all areas of a child's development — it's an essential activity of early childhood. The whole game of school is one in which a child cannot succeed without make-believe! But, I wonder, can anyone succeed in the game of life without make-believe? If you could not make believe, life would be so serious ... or impossible.

Sara Smilansky, professor of child clinical psychology at Tel Aviv University in Israel, is currently a visiting professor at the University of Maryland, College Park. A noted researcher and writer on the topic of dramatic and sociodramatic play, Dr. Smilansky's most recent books are *Facilitating Play: A Medium for Promoting Cognitive, Socio-Emotional, and Academic Development* (Psychosocial and Educational Publications, P.O. Box 2146, Gaithersburg, MD 20886) and *Children's Play and Learning*, co-authored with Edgar Klugman (Teachers College Press).

LEARNING AND GROWING
WITH DRAMATIC PLAY

- **YOUR ROLE IN DRAMATIC PLAY**
- **LEARNING AND GROWING WITH DRAMATIC PLAY: DEVELOPMENTAL CHART**
- **DRAMATIC PLAY WITH CHILDREN WHO HAVE SPECIAL NEEDS**
- **TALKING WITH FAMILIES ABOUT DRAMATIC PLAY**
- **LEARNING THROUGH DRAMATIC PLAY: A MESSAGE TO PARENTS**
- **SETTING THE STAGE FOR DRAMATIC PLAY**

YOUR ROLE
IN DRAMATIC PLAY

Picture life without make-believe. For most of us, the ability to dream, to imagine ourselves in other roles and other places — in the future or the past — is what helps us as adults to make decisions and, at the same time, offers us much creative pleasure. That ability to place ourselves in another role begins in early childhood, in settings like your own.

You play a key role in guiding and developing children's dramatic play by providing time, space, materials, and emotional support. Your respect for the themes and props children devise and your willingness to join in the play from time to time communicates to children that you not only value their dramatic play, but also enjoy pretending.

WHAT DO YOU NEED TO KNOW ABOUT DRAMATIC PLAY?

To make the most of your role, it's important to understand what is at work when children engage in pretend play. The questions and answers that follow offer a "refresher" on key aspects.

■ **Are there different kinds of dramatic play?** Yes. When a child takes on a pretend role alone, this is dramatic play. The activity becomes sociodramatic play when the child interacts with another person who is also in a pretend role. During play, children try on the roles of meaningful adults in their lives — mommies, daddies, doctors, storekeepers, babysitters, teachers, etc. The rules of play come from the child (or in sociodramatic play, the children) and are a reflection of the child's understanding of how different people act.

■ **Where do materials and props fit in?** While materials are often a part of dramatic play, they merely act as accessories in the drama. Children's first concerns are "What can we be?" Younger children may be inspired by props, but older preschoolers might decide to be

PHOTO: SUSAN RICHMAN

firefighters, then look for objects that will help them take on their roles.

■ **What is the value of dramatic play?** Research shows that engaging in dramatic play enhances a child's development in many areas. In other words, the whole child benefits from the ability to pretend. For example:

Social: Role-playing is one way to explore what it feels like to be someone else. It may also be a way to begin to understand the perspective of another, thus enhancing a child's development of empathy. Role-playing can also be a group endeavor. As children coordinate with others to decide on a play theme or to select props, they gain valuable experience in cooperating and sharing. These are skills often valued by peers.

Emotional: Dramatic play allows children to express emotions in safe ways. Through role-playing they can feel and experiment with a sense of power. Acting out a frightening situation can help children feel in control of their fears. Pretending to be the adults in their lives helps children feel powerful and secure.

Cognitive: Many key skills and concepts are enhanced through dramatic play. As children interact, they grow in language skills, and often problem-solving skills are refined. Dramatic play can increase a child's ability to think in creative and abstract ways, an advantage throughout school and life. It can also involve the use of symbols (where one object stands for another) so that later on, visualizing a math problem, a place on a map, or an historical incident will be easier for children who have had this experience.

Physical: Dramatic play often involves manipulating objects, such as dressing and undressing baby or working with tools in a fix-it shop. These fine-motor-type activities, as well as the gross-motor activities children participate in as they pretend, enhance coordination.

For a more detailed analysis of the benefits of dramatic play, see the chart beginning on page 18.

■ **Why do some children seem to pretend better than others?** Young children who come to your program skilled in dramatic play most likely have had a significant play partner — a parent, grandparent, older sibling — who took on pretend roles with the child and communicated by example that not only is it okay to pretend, but it's also a lot of fun.

When children have difficulty pretending, the reason may stem from a home environment where dramatic play may have been considered a frivolous activity. Or, when families are preoccupied with the daily struggle to survive or are coping with stressful situations such as substance abuse, they often lack the time or inclination to be playful with their children. There truly may not be time or a place for children to play.

Whatever the reason, your understanding and sensitivity are vital in encouraging these children to develop the ability to express themselves through dramatic play, and to feel free to do it.

HOW CAN YOU ENCOURAGE DRAMATIC PLAY?

There's much you can do to encourage dramatic play. The following are all important areas:

■ **Let children take the lead.** As you know, young children have rich and fertile imaginations. Dramatic play will develop in creative, enriching ways if children are allowed to experiment and explore without adult direction. Think of yourself as the assistant director and the child as both director and star.

■ **Provide time for satisfying play dramas to develop.** Children need stretches of uninterrupted time — at least 45 minutes — in which to develop dramatic-play themes. If the time is too short, older children will barely get past deciding what they will play and who will play what roles before it is time to move on to a new activity. This may also decrease interest in dramatic play.

How children engage in dramatic play depends not only on their experiences, but on their age and developmental levels. These guidelines can help you gauge the play behaviors of the children in your care.

Two-year-olds may:

■ Play "parallel" to others by doing similar things such as feeding a baby. They may also imitate the play actions of nearby children or adults, but not interact with these players.

■ Use realistic objects to imitate adult behavior they have seen, such as talking on a toy telephone.

■ Be very influenced by the props at hand. The prop itself will be a stimulus for play: Without it, the child may not be as likely to think of the activity. For example, a child sees a broom and so begins to sweep.

■ Repeat the actions involved in a familiar routine over and over, without attempting to expand the actions into a real drama.

■ Make noises or sound effects to accompany their play. For example, a child might sit on a wheel-toy and make car noises.

■ Communicate during pretend play more with gestures and motions than with words.

Three-year-olds may:

■ Take on roles of family members or other familiar people, such as doctors, storekeepers, and bus drivers. A "daddy" may put a baby to bed and warn the baby not to get up.

■ Begin to interact with other children in their roles. A "doctor" may give a "baby" a shot, and "baby" will cry.

■ Begin to give personalities, feelings, and voices to dolls and play animals.

■ Plan their play and gather props ahead of time, then announce what they will pretend to be and do.

■ Create imaginary playmates. This occurs more often alone at home than in group situations.

■ Use language in their roles — talking to each other as they play.
■ Enjoy wearing dress-up clothes and viewing themselves in the mirror.

Four-year-olds may:

■ Take on roles outside those of very familiar people, such as police officers, firefighters, and airplane pilots.
■ Take on more adventurous characters in their play, such as astronauts, monsters, robbers, and superheroes.
■ Make an announcement that this is "just pretend," to assure others, and perhaps themselves, that the scene they are developing is not real.
■ Use abstract objects to represent props they need. For example, blocks become walkie-talkies.
■ Repeat favorite play themes to the exclusion of any others.
■ Take on different voices as they play.
■ Re-enact activities or events they have seen on a field trip.
■ Sustain play for the length of the play period.

Five-year-olds may:

■ Engage in extensive communication, discussing at length what the scene will be, who will do what, what props and dress-up clothes they will use, etc. Children may interrupt their play several times to "adjust the script."
■ Use mime to represent pretend objects or situations, such as opening a door that is not there.
■ Involve several children in their play situations, creating diverse roles.
■ Extend the play situation — even over a period of days. As children become involved in the plot, they may bring in new props from home.
■ Create their own props and signs.
■ Enjoy dictating a story about their play and illustrating it.
■ Enjoy adding to a play theme through books and discussions.

■ **Provide the place and, if needed, the props.** While it would be limiting to think that dramatic play can happen only in one corner of the room, stocking an area with interesting props can spark children's imaginations and encourage dramatic play. Also, leave dramatic-play props out in other areas of your setting and let children know they can move props from one area to another. (For ideas on setting up your environment, turn to "Setting the Stage for Dramatic Play," page 28.)

■ **Pick up on children's interests and then provide subtle ways to help them develop their play scenarios.** As you know, children most often role-play situations that are familiar to them — being at home, going to the store or the doctor's office, etc. Yet their interests are ever growing, and they will often talk about something new and exciting they have heard about or seen (whether in person or on television). When you tune in to children's interests, you're better able to expand upon them. For instance, let's say that one of your children has recently been to the hospital to visit a relative. He tells about his experience at circle time and soon some of the other children are sharing their experiences with hospitals and doctors. You might share a book about a visit to a hospital and place some hospital-type props in your dramatic-play area the

same day, leaving them for the children to discover. If their play develops around the theme, listen and observe for other ways you can help to expand it. (Many of the activity plans in this book can be used to expand on themes that children have brought up themselves.)

Picture books about real places or occupations, special visitors, and inviting children to share their experiences are all ways to enhance children's dramatic play. Field trips offer ideal opportunities to build background experiences. For instance, when children observe the interactions of workers and customers at the post office, a post office drama may evolve naturally.

LEARN BY OBSERVING

Children's dramatic play tells a great deal. The roles children choose, as well as the themes that recur, lend insight into their developmental levels and interests. Children's use of language to initiate and sustain pretend roles — and how their plots unfold — help us gauge their communication abilities. The kinds of frightening situations they tackle through play can suggest particular fears and anxieties.

Try to build observation time into your day. Coordinate with other staff members so that observing in the dramatic-play area becomes a part of your schedule. Here are helpful observation suggestions:

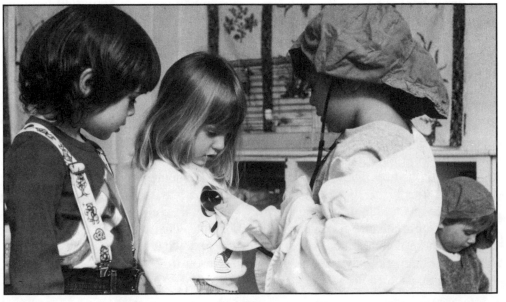

PHOTO: SUPERSTOCK

■ **Watch closely.** There are several elements of play that you can use to assess a child's developmental level.

- Does the child take on a role?
- Does the child use objects and gestures to pretend?
- Is the child interacting with other children in the role and using language?
- Does the child talk about his or her play?
- Does the play episode last at least five minutes, indicating a degree of organization at work?

All of these elements are basic to good sociodramatic play. Take time to jot down anecdotal records to help you get a picture of overall growth. One important caution: Beware of reading too much into children's pretending. As you observe, remember that children are often experimenting with various roles — exploring power and seeing what it might be like. They are also working on understanding complex relationships and events in their own lives, so they may act out or demonstrate more severe behaviors than they have actually experienced. (For additional thoughts, see the sidebar beginning on page 12.)

SHOULD YOU INTERVENE?

Your observations may indicate that particular children are not as skilled as others at dramatic play. Should you intervene, and if so, how?

We know that a child's ability to engage in dramatic play develops with age. But experience is also a factor, and a child who is far less skilled at make-believe than his peers may not socially interact as successfully. There are times when you may want to do more than observe. But even in those situations, follow the child's lead. This means taking on the role of a play partner by getting down on the child's level and commenting nonjudgmentally on something he is doing. As you talk, a dramatic-play theme may become apparent.

For instance, if the child is playing with cars, driving them up and back and up and back, you might say, "Looks like those cars are using a lot of gas. Do you think they might need a fill-up?" From there, if the child says yes, you might enter into pretend play about gas stations. Let the child find the props to use, develop the story line, and decide what role you will take.

There are several ways to sensitively draw a child into more complex, higher-level play. Here are some examples:

■ **Suggest a prop.** Sometimes all that's needed to enhance a child's or group's level of play is a simple prop that relates to their theme. Add a realistic steering wheel to your big block area or a raincoat, boots, and umbrella to the dress-up clothes and see what new and interesting dramas develop.

■ **Suggest a theme.** Pretend-play themes can spring from favorite books, from movies or television programs, from field trips, and, of course, from children's experiences. Listen for experiences that children share with you that can develop into rich and varied dramatic play. For example, when Nathan shares that he and his family had dinner last night at his uncle's pizza parlor, you might encourage other children to share their restaurant experiences. You can either set out a few props to encourage these experiences to develop into a play theme, or suggest that Nathan "open" his own pizza shop near the housekeeping center, and think of props he might need — a telephone and notepad for taking orders, pizzas he might make from modeling clay, an apron, and a sign for his store.

■ **Ask questions.** You can also help children develop or expand their play by asking a few open-ended questions as you take on a role in the play: "What kinds of things can I order to eat at this restaurant?" Just a reminder: With open-ended questions, children should not feel that there is a particular answer you are looking for or a particular way you want them to play. This kind of questioning should help stimulate, not inhibit, children's creativity.

■ **Become a play partner.** As a co-player, you can model dramatic-play techniques. For example, in the course of the play, you might use one object to represent another — making steering motions with a paper plate, or talking into a block as though it's a walkie-talkie. With a child who is ready for a more advanced stage, you might mime an action involving an imaginary prop — drinking an imaginary cup of coffee or steering an imaginary wheel.

■ **Observe rather than assume.** Some children may need help in developing the imaginative potential of a role. Perhaps you observe Susan wearing a firefighter's hat but not engaging in firefighter-type actions. First, give Susan a chance to explain what she's doing. It may not seem firefighter-like to you, but may be perfectly logical to her. If she seems at a loss as to how to proceed with her role, you might suggest a situation: "I'm so glad you're a firefighter, because there is a big fire over here! What should we do to put it out?" If Susan does not respond to this prompt, you might offer to help her hold the "hose" while she puts out the fire.

CHILD'S PLAY:
SENSITIVE ISSUES

Dramatic play offers children one of the safest and most appropriate ways to understand the world and their place in it. It also provides a window through which a caring adult can glimpse profound issues that concern a child. Yet, sometimes what you see — or think you see — through that window may be troubling. What should a teacher do when children act out sexual roles, when a pretend "disciplining" of a doll seems to verge on abuse, or when role-playing "family life" includes drinking or taking drugs?

WHAT DOES THIS PLAY MEAN?

One of the most challenging aspects of this kind of play is determining its significance. Play involving sensitive themes does not automatically signal a real-life problem. In fact, be cautious of reading too much into children's pretend play. Children are experimenting with roles, often adult roles of power and control. They may be demonstrating behaviors different from those they have experienced themselves.

Children are also very keen observers. Sometimes adults may fail to realize how much a child is taking in during a family disagreement or an adult get-together. Children may also observe activities on television that are adult in nature, especially if viewing habits are not carefully monitored. And, sometimes children stumble onto activities — like opening an unlocked bedroom door — that they were never meant to see. So, taken together, there is great potential for sensitive play scenarios that are basically innocent in origin.

On the other hand, this kind of play, if it occurs with frequency, may signal a problem in a child's environment or development. That is why it cannot be ignored.

The important thing to remember when dealing with sensitive play themes is that the issue is not whether what the child is struggling to understand through play is good or bad, acceptable or unacceptable. What's important is how to help the child with issues being expressed.

THINK AHEAD

The best way to handle sensitive moments in the dramatic-play area is to be prepared for the possibility that they will occur. Part of being prepared involves thinking about your own feelings. When children play out their understanding of such topics as adult sexual behavior, divorce, or death, adults may bring their own unresolved conflicts to the situations. As an observer, make sure you don't react in ways that might make a child feel guilty or ashamed. Take time to evaluate whether this play is a cause for concern and has a relationship to reality.

Also take time to analyze your own feelings. Think back to the way adults responded to you as a child when you had questions about sex, death, drinking, or drugs. Evaluate whether the response helped support your self-

▪ **Model how to interact with others in pretend roles.** Naturally, children don't need to always interact, but if you observe that a child almost never engages in sociodramatic play, you may want to involve him or her in scenarios that may interest others. For instance, if you see José playing with a pretend steering wheel, you might ask, "Is this the bus to Boston? I need to get there. How much will it cost?" Then invite one or two children to come along for the ride. Encourage José to interact with the other "passengers" through open-ended questions.

You can also model roles through parallel play. If Brian is just holding a doll, you might sit next to him with a doll of your own and ask, "Are you that baby's daddy? He's so cute. Is he hungry? My baby is hungry. I think I will feed my baby now."

▪ **Encourage the use of language.** Help children who are not yet verbal by narrating their actions: "Shanelle is cooking. What are you making? Oh, I can smell it. It smells good." With older children, you might encourage verbal activities such as talking on the telephone. When appropriate to the play, you might "hear" the phone ring in the house area, answer it, and hand it to a child saying, "It's for you." After the

concept and gave you the answers you needed. Use your own experiences to help shape responses that will be truly supportive and nonjudgmental.

Play that may involve sexual and/or substance abuse is another matter. You need to observe closely, and avoid reacting in ways that might make the child feel guilty. Decide with your director what course you should take in investigating the child's situation more closely.

A SCENARIO TO CONSIDER

Let's look at a way to handle a delicate situation such as one involving sex. Picture this: You hear giggles in the housekeeping center but no children are in sight. Upon investigating, you find four-year-old Kirk on top of four-year-old Ellie. You calmly ask what the children are playing, and Kirk explains that this is what his mommy and her boyfriend do at night after he has gone to bed.

Here's one way to respond: You sit next to the children, remembering that it's important to avoid developing any sense of guilt or shame, and at the same time, help them understand that this particular play is not appropriate. You might say, "I'm glad the two of you are friends. What are some other things that friends do together?" Find an activity that the pair seems particularly interested in, and help them get involved. When they are engaged in the more appropriate play, withdraw, but maintain an observing eye.

Depending on your comfort level, you can also sit with an arm around each and explain that when grown-ups behave in the way they were playing, it's because the adults like each other very much. (Depending on the "rules" you have set up in your program, you might also add, "Remember, in our room, a person's body is his or her own, and not something for other people to touch.") Then ask the children if they like each other a lot and use their response to start a discussion of various ways friends show they like each other, such as exchanging hugs, painting a picture for a buddy, or sitting together for music, story, or snack. Finish by guiding the pair to try one of these expressions of friendship, perhaps by helping them get set up in the art area.

SEEK SUPPORT OF EXPERTS

With some issues, you may want to seek professional guidance to determine the significance of the behavior. Pediatricians, mental-health experts, social workers, and other specialists in your community are all people you can turn to for advice.

Books for adults and children on sensitive issues can be another source of assistance. For example, *When a Pet Dies* by Fred Rogers is a wonderful book to use to help children understand a beloved pet's death or to just open up the topic of death and dying for questions and discussion. Consult with the librarian in your school or public library for help in finding these resources.

Even the most "shock-proof" teacher can be unnerved by some activities that are played out in the classroom. But, by preparing for the possibility of these events, remembering that children are only working out their own questions about these issues in the way that is most available to them, and by drawing on the variety of resources that are available to you, you can help children gain a healthy understanding of some of life's most complex issues.

Edgar Klugman, Ed.D., is professor of early childhood education at Wheelock College. He collaborated with his wife **Hertha Klugman**, a free-lance writer specializing in children's issues.

conversation, inquire, "Who was that? What did he/she want?" (Be careful that this kind of interaction doesn't interrupt children's play.)

DEFUSING POTENTIAL PROBLEMS WITHOUT INTERFERING WITH CREATIVITY

Conflicts do arise during dramatic play. There may be minor disagreements or major shouting matches. There may be situations where children are engaged in play that leads to injuries. Understanding how to enter play situations to help defuse potential problems, and also how to withdraw, will help you keep dramatic play safe and stimulating.

The examples that follow highlight two ways to intervene in minor problem situations without interfering with children's creativity. For help with more intense conflicts resulting from superhero or weapon play, see "Power Play," page 16.

■ **Safer Play.** At the sand table, four-year-olds Jacob and Maria giggle and hoot with surprise as they pour sand from various vessels onto one another's

DRAMATIC PLAY
WITH
MIXED AGE GROUPS

A family child-care home is the ideal setting for young children's dramatic play. Here, children are exposed to a variety of real props for acting out family roles and routines. As a natural part of their day, children observe activities such as cooking and caring for younger children. Working with a smaller number of children also means that you can observe dramatic play more easily and look for ways to enhance and extend it.

Of course, there are challenges. With a small group of children comprised of mixed ages and abilities, facilitating dramatic play can be difficult. Here are ways to help you and your children enjoy dramatic play:

■ *Build on everyday experiences.* Encourage children to observe when the garbage truck comes, when you fix lunch, when you make out a shopping list, etc. These routine activities can spark young imaginations, particularly if you supply appropriate props such as work gloves and trash bags, pots and pans, modeling clay, and

paper and crayons.

■ *Look for ways to involve younger children in complementary roles.* Don't look for twos and young threes to join in the group, but help this age find their own ways to be part of the fun. For example, when the group is playing house, a toddler might care for a baby doll.

■ *Support cooperation.* As children get to know each other, they are better able to cooperate on play themes and involve everyone in a scenario. Eventually, your whole group might run a household or be pirates on a ship.

■ *Establish a consistent routine.* Set specific times for free play, lunch, nap, stories, etc., so children can expect a certain time for dramatic play.

■ *Store props with children in mind.* To encourage independent play and cleanup, let children know which household items they may use for play, where those items are found, and where to return them. For example, dishes for play might be stored on the bottom shelf of a kitchen cupboard. Mark both the cupboard door and the

hands and pretend that their hands are hiding. Then they quickly pull their hands out of hiding. Cliff, their teacher, stands nearby and watches the play. He's concerned that flying sand may pose a safety hazard, yet he fears that directly intervening may deflate the pair's joy in their play and discourage any natural elaboration. Cliff quietly positions himself at an empty space at the table. He buries a few plastic props, creating big sand mounds over the hidden treasures. Then he burrows his hands into the mounds and retrieves the items. Jacob and Maria are quickly intrigued by Cliff's form of sand play.

shelf with dish shapes so children can find and return dishes after play.

■ *Be a saver.* Almost anything can be used for children's dramatic play — empty paper towel tubes, old clothes, pots and pans, etc. Check each item to be sure it's safe for children. Wash or clean the item, and find a place to store it.

■ *Make sure your environment is safe for play.* Children often like to seek out small spaces — under tables, behind couches, etc. Check that all electrical cords are secured to outlets, and open electrical sockets are safely capped. Be sure there is nothing on tables that could fall on children.

■ *Protect your environment.* Some simple rules and cleanup aids can help protect your furnishings. For example, messy play in water or a pan of sand should be done outdoors. When bad weather keeps you indoors, place a plastic tablecloth under pans and tables.

■ *Supervise.* Observing children's dramatic play is important, not only to understand their interests and involvement but also to watch for problems — toddlers putting objects in their mouths, older children "fixing" walls and windows with hammers, etc.

Kathie Spitzley, a family day-care provider in Holland, Michigan, for 10 years, is accredited by the National Association of Family Day Care.

Soon they are burying and retrieving, squealing with delight at each discovery. Cliff quietly leaves. Without decreasing their fun, he has successfully directed their play to a safer process.

■ **When Players and Plot Ideas Clash.** At the outdoor climber several five-year-olds are acting out their own version of "The Three Pigs." Max, playing the wolf, pretends to "huff and puff and blow the house (climber) down." The other children squirm and squeal in delighted fear. But suddenly a conflict arises. Max insists the house is made of straw and can be blown down. The others insist it's made of bricks and can't be. Soon a shouting match begins. Clarisse, the children's family day-care provider, hears the commotion and moves closer. Deciding that their happy play might be disintegrating, she gently asks, "What could the wolf do if the house is made of bricks?" The children stop shouting and start to think, while Clarisse remains silent, giving the children time to suggest their own solutions. One child calls out, "He could climb down the chimney!" Max agrees that's a good solution. The conflict is over as he scrambles to the top of the climber and pretends to lower himself into the chimney. As the play resumes, Clarisse walks to the other side of the playground, where she keeps an eye on the players. Her subtle intervention defused a conflict and helped these fives find a solution that is acceptable to all.

In each situation, key elements in the adult's behavior contributed to a subtle redirection of play that resolved the problem. These behaviors include:

■ Listening and observing before taking any action

■ Timing involvement so that it does not interrupt natural creative flows

■ Modeling play options but not imposing them on children

■ Letting children in conflict find their own solutions to problems

■ Respecting children's ideas and creative expression.

POWER PLAY

There may not be guns or other weapons among the available toys in your program, yet you see children using blocks or their fingers to shoot pretend foes. You may discourage superhero play, yet young Batman still leaps across the playground "ka-powing" imaginary criminals. Why, whether prohibited or not, does aggressive play creep into children's pretend play?

TRYING OUT POWER

Pretending to dominate or injure are ways for children to experiment with power. By shooting an animal, conquering a scary monster, or taking control of someone else, children become powerful players. Often, they are trying to gain control over frightening situations.

Superhero play is also a "quest" for power. By dubbing himself or herself "Superperson," a four-year-old instantaneously becomes an awesome presence. When you consider how little power young children experience in their everyday lives, the appeal of power and control becomes apparent.

Naturally, in an increasingly violent world it's disquieting to see children mirror violence in their play. However, it's important to remember that children have their own perceptions of violence and death. In children's play, when a character is killed, there's usually a way to bring that character back to life — through a potion, chant, or other means of imagination.

For most young children, aggressive play is essentially natural and harmless. Telling children that this kind of play is wrong may make them feel guilty for having normal emotions such as anger, frustration, and fear, and they will not understand why this play is wrong. At the same time, it may also stifle creativity.

DISARM WEAPON PLAY

There are ways to redirect weapon play into more pro-social activities without making children feel guilty. Begin by observing. A child may resort to using a weapon because she hasn't thought of anything else to do. Gently challenge the child to think of different ways to escape her foe by brainstorming together. Or step into the play and suggest that the scary dinosaur be brought under control by a friendlier character. Encourage the child to devise activities that the pretend creature might enjoy.

Children may also use weapons when they're struggling with strong emotions. In these tense moments, a child may stop pretending and use a

weapon to hurt another child. While you want to acknowledge that anger and frustration are normal emotions, the child must understand that it is not okay to work out those feelings by hurting others. Here are ways to intercede when children use weapons in anger:

▪ **Encourage a child to verbalize his feelings.** "You're angry, aren't you? Did the monster do something to make you mad? Use words to tell the monster why you are angry."

PHOTO: © ERIKA STONE 1987

■ **Be direct about why a child cannot hurt others.** "You're angry, aren't you? But I can't let you use this weapon, even if you're just pretending. David is a real person, and it hurts him when you hit him with this block. Use words to tell David what you want him to do."

■ **Offer safe alternatives for working through anger in a physical way.** "You feel like hitting, don't you? Here's a pillow (or some clay) you can pound as much as you want."

HELP SUPERHEROES EXIST PEACEFULLY

Superhero play is often accompanied by exuberance and camaraderie, which are wonderful emotions for children to explore and experience. The key to managing this kind of play is finding ways to highlight the positive qualities while discouraging weapons and other negative elements.

The suggestions for controlling weapon play can be useful for disarming superheroes, too. When superhero play frightens other children, designate a play area just for superheroes. Or set a rule that when children hear a special bell, superheroes lose their powers. Ring it if you see play is getting out of control. Try these ideas, which will also enhance language and creative development:

■ **Talk about superheroes.** At circle time, ask volunteers to describe their favorite characters.

■ **Invite children to make up a story about a favorite superhero.** Record the story, then play it back.

■ **Ask children to create their own superhero.** What is the hero's name? What does the hero look like, and what are his or her special powers? Invite children to draw or paint their hero to show others.

STUCK IN THE SUPERHERO RUT?

What should you do when a child engages in superhero or weapon play — or superhero play with weapons — almost exclusively?

Observe the child. He may pretend to shoot or attack when he can't think of anything else to do. If the child is not adept at dramatic play, he may fall back on familiar roles because he's not sure how to take on others. It is also possible that the child enjoys more daring themes and finds those of his peers uninteresting. For each cause, here are ways to help:

■ **When a child needs alternatives, engage him in creative brainstorming.** Say, "What are some ways you could get away from the monster without shooting him?"

■ **If the problem is lack of dramatic-play skills, observe the group's play themes and look for roles that a less adept player might take on.** Quietly suggest these roles to the child and group.

■ **If superhero play is the result of boredom, try to encourage adventure themes.** For instance, you might set out a large appliance carton and ask children what it could be, or suggest — never force — the idea of using it as a boat to play shipwreck. Then encourage the child and others to look for props.

KEEP YOUR PERSPECTIVE

Aggressive play is understandably troubling to observe, but try to maintain your perspective. In most cases, children are not really trying to hurt one another. They are looking for ways to feel powerful and in control, to overcome their fears and frustrations, or to feel less overwhelmed by their world. Your understanding and guidance is essential.

Adapted from "Should Superheroes Be Expelled From Preschool?" by Marilyn Segal (*Pre-K Today*, October 1987) and from "Weapon Play" by Sandra Waite-Stupiansky, Ph.D. (*Pre-K Today*, October 1989).

LEARNING AND GROWING

Dramatic play opens up doors of wonder, enchantment, courage, and fun for young children. Yet it is far from simply an imaginative experience. While creative development is enhanced through pretend play, so are social, emotional, physical, and cognitive development. Literally every aspect of development is enhanced when children engage in dramatic play.

This five-page chart illustrates the versatility of dramatic play and how it can contribute to developing the whole child. Share it with staff and with children's families.

Each entry begins with a description of how a specific skill or concept is developed through dramatic play. "Ways to Assist" are suggestions for promoting further development. "Developmental Considerations" help you know what to expect from younger (ages 2-3) and older (ages 4-5) preschoolers.

Naturally, behavior varies greatly at all ages. What individual children gain from pretend play depends on factors such as age, whom they play with, materials they use, and even the themes they choose. View this chart as a source of guidelines only.

PHOTO: SUSAN RICHMAN

WITH DRAMATIC PLAY

EXPRESSING EMOTIONS

Because children are "just pretending," it is safe for them to express a range of emotions during dramatic play. They might be a comforting parent, a crying baby, or an angry monster. Pretend play also offers children ways to "work through" stressful life situations.

Ways to Assist

- Encourage children to express emotions in their play. Remember, showing emotion, including anger, sadness, and fear, is healthy, but children may need guidance in learning acceptable ways.
- When reading to children, discuss how a character feels: "How do you think Corduroy felt when he thought no one loved him?"
- Listen for the emotions that children express, but be careful about reading too much into what you hear. Use common sense and your own experience to help you balance your concern.

Developmental Considerations

- Younger children have trouble sorting through strong emotions. They may resort to tantrums because they lack the words to describe how they feel. Pretend play can help them learn more acceptable ways to express their feelings.
- Older children sometimes use pretend play to sort out their emotions. Because they can verbalize their emotions, they will often pretend to feel anger, happiness, fear, and sadness as part of play.

DEVELOPING AUTONOMY

Dramatic play can help children feel confident and in control. They can replay frightening situations in the role of the person with power, such as the doctor who gives the shot. And, by deciding their own play themes and using props in their own way, children explore and experiment with roles as they develop confidence in their own ideas and abilities.

Ways to Assist

- Your role is one of assistant, *always* letting children take the lead. If you see a way to enhance a theme, do so subtly by assuming a role or by asking a question that may spur ideas.
- Weapon-like objects give some children feelings of power. Redirect play by brainstorming other ways to deal with foes, acknowledging — *not* covering up — children's fears and emotions.
- When children have endured a stressful situation, provide props to help them work through their emotions from a position of power.

Developmental Considerations

- Autonomy is an emotional milestone for younger children. If they don't achieve it, as they get older they may shy away from new challenges. Make sure your play environment is a safe place to take risks, so that children can experiment and feel in control.
- Older children's initiative can be misinterpreted as defiance, as in a child who turns off the room lights for nighttime play. As you work on compromises, remember to respect children's natural need for power.

DISTINGUISHING FANTASY FROM REALITY

Learning to distinguish between fantasy and reality is an important developmental step. Dramatic play helps children learn to differentiate between the two. It gives children the license and the means to pretend and lets them experiment with a variety of roles — some based on real life, like family members, and some on purely fantasy characters like super-heroes and monsters. In time, the boundary between what is real and what is make-believe becomes clearer.

Ways to Assist

- Accept children's play themes without questioning their realism.
- Play along with a fantasy. If a child magically turns you into a baby, take on the role.
- If you are not sure how to participate in a fantasy situation, ask the child what to do: "What should I do with this magic flower potion?"

Developmental Considerations

- Younger children slip in and out of fantasies. They cannot verbalize a change to a fantasy situation, but their actions may signal the change.
- Most older children know what is real and what is pretend in their play. They can explain the ideas behind their fantasies and may stop fantasizing to take on the role of director: "Now pretend that her clothes turn into rags because the clock struck twelve."

LEARNING AND GROWING

FINE-MOTOR SKILLS

When children change baby's clothes, make play money to use in a store, dial the telephone for a pretend chat, or write down an order at a play restaurant, they are practicing fine-motor control. Dramatic play offers many opportunities to develop fine-motor skills — those skills that will later enable children to hold a pencil and write letters, numbers, words, etc.

Ways to Assist
- Set out plenty of materials children can use to make their own props, such as bills and coins, price tags, signs, and labels.
- Provide writing materials like notepads and markers for children to use in their play.
- To help children whose fine-motor skills have not yet developed, use Velcro fasteners on baby and dress-up clothes.

Developmental Considerations
- Younger children are developing fine-motor skills continually. By ages two and three, they should be able to use each hand independently, such as holding a cup in a one and a cracker in another. (Activities involving eye-hand coordination require great effort and can be frustrating if too advanced for this age.)
- Older children are developing mastery of many crucial fine-motor tasks, such as buttoning clothing, drawing, cutting, and pasting — activities they will do with much greater control after age five.

ROLE-TAKING

Dramatic play offers children a safe environment for imitating actions they observe in everyday life, trying out roles they associate with power, and exploring their fears. This role-taking is an important part of beginning to learn about and understand their worlds and the people in them.

Ways to Assist
- Collect a variety of props that will suggest different roles for children to play.
- Help children put themselves into a character's role: "How does a doctor help a sick baby?"
- Guide children who tend to play the same roles to try others. If Eliza is always the mother, be it mother mouse or mother dinosaur, suggest she play the baby dinosaur or the cat who sneaks up on the mice.
- Encourage discussion of roles. "Jack's a daddy, and he's cooking. Who else's daddy cooks? What does he make?"

Developmental Considerations
- Young children take on the roles of others by enacting familiar routines like driving a car, rocking a baby, or pouring tea. They may repeat these isolated routines but rarely develop them into a "story."
- Older children develop extended play episodes and involve their characters in a variety of situations. They play roles with accuracy, talking and acting like the characters.

PERSPECTIVE-TAKING

Role-playing lets children see a given situation from another point of view, an essential step in moral development. While their understanding of many roles is unsophisticated, children are far more able to develop empathy when they have experienced different roles.

Ways to Assist
- Encourage children to share their feelings when others upset them: "Jorge, tell Maria how you feel when she grabs your baby." Children often need to be reminded that others have feelings, too.
- At moments when questions will not intrude on play, ask children about the feelings of characters they are playing: "How does the mommy feel when her children won't go to sleep?"
- As you read stories, encourage children to put themselves in a character's place: "How would you feel if you were Jack and your beans grew like that?"

Developmental Considerations
- Younger children begin to take the perspective of others in simple ways, such as by wailing like a baby or offering comfort as a parent. As this stage ends, they talk for their characters, such as speaking for both a baby and parent.
- Older children are more aware that others have wants and needs which may be different from their own. As this understanding grows, they begin to coordinate their needs with those of others, making cooperative play possible.

WITH DRAMATIC PLAY

COOPERATING AND SHARING

Dramatic play gives children a setting for learning about interacting with others, such as how to enter a play situation and add to the play. Successful interaction requires children to learn to give and take, and to take on various kinds of roles. In the process, they learn essential life skills, such as the ability to compromise.

Ways to Assist

■ Coach a child in ways to enter a group: "Meg, let's ask them what they're playing, and if you may play, too."
■ Brainstorm with a child to find an ancillary role to add to a play situation in progress. "Monae, could you be another shopper at this store?"
■ When children disagree, ask questions that will help them resolve the problems on their own: "Yusef and Kim, what can you do so that both of you can play with the truck?"

Developmental Considerations

■ Younger preschoolers are still very egocentric and may enter a play situation by taking props that others are using. Cooperative play will be rare. You might assist a child by suggesting a parallel play situation — such as having the child care for a baby next to other twos or threes who are playing parent and baby.
■ Older preschoolers are more aware of the rights of others but still can be egocentric. They will need your occasional guidance to play cooperatively.

MULTICULTURAL AWARENESS

Play themes such as family life can bring out similarities and differences between children's cultural backgrounds. Peers may pretend to cook and eat a variety of foods. They may give different kinds of roles to pretend mommies and daddies. Dramatic play becomes a means of helping children learn to accept and appreciate other children's customs and lifestyles, and understand that diversity is natural and good.

Ways to Assist

■ Start by providing props specific to the cultures of your children. Later, add props from other cultures to encourage multicultural play themes and activities.
■ Focus on similarities among peoples, such as the common need for food, clothing, shelter, and love. Encourage discussion when children question differences: "Not everyone eats the same food for breakfast. Let's all share what we eat."
■ Read nonbiased books involving a variety of cultures.
■ Model respect for diversity through your words and actions.

Developmental Considerations

■ Younger children tend to think that everyone is like them. They may ask about differences, but usually in nonjudgmental ways.
■ Older children enjoy learning about other cultures. However, they may repeat hurtful comments without recognizing the impact of what they are saying.

CREATIVE THINKING

Creativity involves thinking about situations or materials in novel ways. Dramatic play is an ideal setting in which creative thinking can flourish. Children use their imaginations to be anyone and anywhere, then use props to enhance those themes. Even the rules of play come from their own imaginations.

Ways to Assist

■ Expose children to imaginative characters and events by sharing good children's books.
■ Contribute to an imaginary situation as a play partner: "Look! Here comes an elephant!"
■ Encourage children to describe imaginary play situations they construct so others can join in.
■ Never judge a theme as "silly" or tell a child, "That couldn't happen." Let them know they have the power to create, change, and undo imaginary events.
■ Invite children to draw pictures or dictate stories about play themes to expand their creativity into other outlets.

Developmental Considerations

■ Younger children will vary in their level of creativity. It can be enhanced by watching older children model creative thinking and by having their creative attempts acknowledged and encouraged by adults.
■ Older children need supportive adults and a variety of options to make the most of their creative potential. They need to express creativity through a variety of outlets.

LEARNING AND GROWING WITH DRAMATIC PLAY

COGNITIVE DEVELOPMENT

UNDERSTANDING SYMBOLS

When children use a toy, an abstract object, or a gesture to represent something else, they are learning to use symbols. This means the child is able to take on a mental image of an object that is not there. Developing an understanding of symbols is an important step in the process of learning to read and compute because it enables children to recognize that letters and numbers stand for something.

Ways to Assist
■ Encourage younger children to use "pretend" objects when an appropriate prop is not available. You may need to model this — how to use two fingers to simulate scissors in a barber shop or how to pretend to give money to the "bus driver."
■ Pretend together through finger-plays, chants, and music. Remember, when children use hand or body motions to act out a song, they are learning to represent events through symbolic gestures.
■ Invite children to use written symbols to describe their play by dictating stories for you to transcribe.

Developmental Considerations
■ Younger children are very literal in their use of props. They use an object for its intended purpose and often get their ideas for play from the props at hand.
■ Older children tend to be more imaginative in their use of props. They will substitute one object for another or will mime a prop if one is not available.

PROBLEM-SOLVING SKILLS

Dramatic play offers a rich variety of problems to solve — a needed prop is not available so a substitute must be found, two children want to play the same role, a child making a sail for her boat must try several materials before finding one that works, etc. Learning to solve problems is critical to all areas of life and, as you know, children are never too young to begin to develop problem-solving skills.

Ways to Assist
■ Guide children in learning the following steps in solving a problem:
 •Identify the problem: We need space helmets for our moon trip.
 •Brainstorm several solutions: What can we use?
 •Choose the solution that seems the best and try it out.
 •Evaluate the idea: Is this a good space helmet? Should we try another way to make a helmet?
 •Support children's attempts at problem-solving, even when their solutions seem illogical. Trial and error is a good teacher.

Developmental Considerations
■ Younger children are easily overwhelmed by too many options. When there's a problem to solve, offer two solutions and let them choose.
■ Older children may need help going through the steps to solve a problem. Some may struggle with decisions and become frustrated if they are rushed. Give children plenty of chances to solve their own problems, because these skills grow with practice.

LANGUAGE SKILLS

Dramatic play helps children understand the power of language. Through play, they learn that words give them the means to communicate ideas, and to organize props and even peers. Dramatic play also helps children develop language as they try out words and phrases modeled by peers and adults. When children use labels in play, they begin to make the connection between spoken and written language.

Ways to Assist
■ Observe and comment nonjudgmentally on younger children's play to help them attach words to their actions: "Carrie is washing the dishes now."
■ As you pick up on children's interests, use vocabulary related to specific themes.
■ Provide writing materials like pads and markers for children to use in their play. Encourage them to make signs for restaurants or shops.
■ If you are assuming a role, ask children questions to encourage them to talk about their play: "What kind of doctor are you, Shameeka?"

Developmental Considerations
■ Younger children are learning to use language, so they tend to speak in words and phrases: "Car go." Help children develop vocabulary by expanding those phrases: "Are you making the car go?"
■ Older children have the language skills to carry on involved dialogs. They talk for characters and verbalize ideas for developing a theme.

Sandra Waite-Stupiansky, Ph.D., is an assistant professor at the Center for Teacher Education at the State University of New York at Plattsburgh.

DRAMATIC PLAY WITH CHILDREN WHO HAVE SPECIAL NEEDS

Children with special needs gain from dramatic play in every way that nondisabled children do. In fact, the experience may be even more enriching for special-needs children, who have often been protected by adults and may have had limited opportunities to interact with other children. Sociodramatic play gives them the opportunity to feel the power of adult roles, while also developing key social skills such as taking turns, sharing, and cooperating.

HELPING CHILDREN WITH SOCIAL PLAY

Even if they are developmentally ready for cooperative play, children with special needs may not respond to those who approach them. And, some children may hesitate to invite a peer who looks or acts differently to take part in a dramatic-play theme. Consequently, it's often necessary for you to actively promote interaction.

■ **Teach nondisabled children how to approach their special-needs peers.** First and foremost, set a tone of acceptance of diversity so that children will be more understanding of the differences they see in their disabled peers. Then show children how to bring a special-needs peer into a play group, such as by taking the child's hand and offering him or her props to use.

■ **Help the special-needs child find appropriate ways to enter play.** Coach the child in social skills that will make her a more appealing play partner to peers. Help by suggesting simple but appropriate language for entering a play group, such as "May I play, too?" Urge the child to look at peers when speaking and to respond to questions or greetings. When play has ended, review positive social interactions you observed: "Joel and George shared the cash register. Ivan and Mary took good care of their baby together."

■ **Join in as a play partner and model.** Another way to help a special-needs child become more adept at dramatic play is by modeling how to play with others. Take an active role and engage the child as a play partner. As much as possible, let the child take the lead, suggesting the play theme. As she becomes comfortable in a role-play situation, invite another child to join in your play. Eventually you'll want to find a reason for your character to exit the scene.

ENCOURAGE PLAY ON MANY LEVELS

Naturally, you want children to play at the level they're best able to handle, so your dramatic-play area should be well-stocked with familiar items such as cooking utensils and housekeeping equipment. But to help children grow in their dramatic-play skills, encourage them to take part in more challenging play themes. For example, if a child seems ready, look for a subordinate role that he or she might fill in a higher-level play session. For example, the child might be a patient during hospital play or the one who bags the groceries during store play. By taking a minor role, the child can observe firsthand the more sophisticated play of her peers, who can help direct the child's actions.

EVERY CHILD IS SPECIAL

Different kinds and levels of disability will effect a child's degree of experience and success. Parents and therapists can give the best information and advice about working with specific children. However, the general tips that follow offer guidance in helping children with different kinds of special needs increase their dramatic-play skills.

■ **Children with visual impairments**
During dramatic play a child applies observations of the world to pretend scenarios. When a child lacks the ability to observe, dramatic play is less likely to be part of her play routine. Visually impaired children generally begin dramatic play at a later age than nondisabled peers and are less imaginative in their play. A visually impaired child needs a lot of help and encouragement to become comfortable and adept at dramatic play.

How you can help:
• Familiarize the child with the dramatic-play area. Let her examine the play props and try to guess their identities. Explain the location of each object in the center. Discuss what each object is used for and various features of the item: "This is a refrigerator. It has doors that open. Feel for the handle and open it. Feel the shelves that food is put on."
• As much as possible, stock the center with props that have texture and are easy to manipulate. A toy corn-on-the-cob, for example, should have deep grooves separating the kernels that will help the child identify it quickly. Large objects are easier to handle.
• Once play begins, ask others to explain the plot to the visually impaired child: "We are playing store. Here is the cash register. You pay here." Stay nearby, and, if necessary, explain what to do: "Hold out your cup so Sean can pour you a drink."
• Remind nondisabled peers to use the child's name and make sure they have the child's attention before speaking.

Encourage them to explain what is going on as the action develops and to use labels for objects — *cup, hat* — rather than pronouns — *this, it*.

■ **Children with hearing impairments**
Listening is an effort for hearing-impaired children, which means they may avoid highly verbal activities like sociodramatic play. A child may choose to engage in dramatic play by playing parent to a baby doll, for example, and may even play alongside others. But a hearing-impaired child will usually need help in becoming a part of group sociodramatic play.

How you can help:
• Depending on the child's language abilities, help by suggesting appropriate ways to join in group play themes. This may range from reviewing socially appropriate phrases, such as, "May I play, too?" to demonstrating a polite tap on the shoulder to get the attention of a group member.
• If the child's verbal skills are limited, look for nonverbal roles the child can assume, such as a sleeping baby, an animal in a zoo, or a silent mail sorter in the post office. Encourage the child's nondisabled peers to create roles that require more action than talk.
• To facilitate lip-reading, make sure that the lighting in the dramatic-play area is good. Then remind the child to look directly at others and to concentrate on what they say. Remind nondisabled children to look directly at the child or to touch the child when addressing her.

■ **Children with physical impairments**
Physically impaired children have a limited ability to interact with their environment. As a result, they bring fewer experiences to dramatic play. Because of their limited mobility, they may not feel as able to take part in group situations as other children.

How you can help:
• Adapt the dramatic-play area so that it will be safer and more comfortable for a physically impaired child. Furniture that is heavy and stable will give the child

something to lean on without falling. Weigh down movable toys like wagons and doll carriages so they'll be less likely to tip over if the child pushes them. Allow for wide aisles between furniture and avoid area rugs.

• If the child uses a mechanical aid like a wheelchair, walker, cane, or crutches, discuss safety rules such as not laying crutches on the floor where others can trip over them.

• Nondisabled children may tend to assign the child secondary roles. While minor roles may be appropriate as the child is getting used to group sociodramatic play, the child should gradually be involved in more primary roles to develop dramatic-play skills. Help the group adapt props or roles so that the child is a major part of the action.

■ **Children with mental retardation**
These children play at a level consistent with their mental age. A four-year-old with a mental age of 30 months will play like a two-and-half-year-old. Mentally retarded children also tend to be rigid in their play — repeating the same roles over and over. They depend heavily on props and may not think of sweeping, for example, if a broom is not present. They tend to use props only for their designated purpose and rarely substitute one prop for another, such as calling a stick a broom. Consequently, it's hard for a child who is functioning at a lower, less-imaginative level to join in the play of same-age peers.
How you can help:
• When a group is involved in a dramatic-play situation that is above the child's level, set up a second dramatic-play setting nearby, perhaps by acting as a play partner to the child.
• Use modeling to encourage the child to try different play themes from those she usually chooses. Draw the child's attention to peers using props in imaginative ways, and model substituting one prop for another.
• Change is difficult for a mentally retarded child. Alert the child five to ten minutes before the end of playtime that she will soon need to clean up and put away play props. If the child has been playing with a group, give her a specific job to do during cleanup, such as putting away the spoons.

■ **Children with behavior disturbances**
These children commonly display one of three types of extreme behavior: withdrawal, aggression, or hyperactivity. Any of these behaviors can interfere with sociodramatic play.
How you can help:
• Start simple. Too much stimulation can lead to increased extremes in behavior. You might start as the child's play partner, gradually try to interest one or two other children in joining the play, and then step out.
• Children who are withdrawn need lots of time to become comfortable with a dramatic-play activity. Let the child begin by watching from outside the area, and then by standing among the others as they play. Set up a second dramatic-play area next to the ongoing one that is related but different.
• Try pairing a child who is aggressive with a more mature, understanding child. Review the rules of the dramatic-play area with the child, helping her find a role to play and props to use: "Kyle, why don't you sweep the floor of your house with this broom?" When signs of aggression do appear, help the child realize that she is upset, and talk about positive ways to handle these feelings. Offer lots of reinforcement when the child behaves well.
• Children who are hyperactive may have difficulty maintaining the attention needed for participating in peers' extended play themes. Play alongside the child if this helps her pay attention longer. Suggest new and expanded plot ideas when the child becomes restless.
• Transitions can be stressful for children with behavior problems. Alert the children close to cleanup time so that they can prepare for a change in activity, then stay close to be of help.

Merle Karnes, Ed.D., is a professor of special education at the University of Illinois at Urbana.

TALKING WITH FAMILIES
ABOUT DRAMATIC PLAY

Most adults understand intuitively that dramatic play is a healthy and delightful activity for children. Just consider the kinds of toys we often give children: stuffed animals, dolls, play dishes, and cars and trucks. Add to those props a family member's willingness to string up a blanket tent for a pretend campout or to be the patient of a pint-sized doctor, and you have critical home-based support for dramatic play.

Why then might you find yourself explaining why dramatic play is an important part of your program? Many adults see dramatic play as just play — fun, but not "learning." Unschooled in the ways in which dramatic play enhances development, concerned family members may not appreciate the social, emotional, cognitive, physical, and creative gains that a child can make through pretending. The challenge, then, is to help family members recognize how children learn through dramatic play and how it benefits a child's total development. This sampling of ideas can help:

■ **Read All About It!** Does your program send home a newsletter? Include a section on dramatic play. Tell families about some of the play themes children are enjoying and suggest ways they can expand on those themes at home. In each edition, highlight a particular skill or area of development that's enhanced through dramatic play.

■ **Great Performances.** If a picture is worth a thousand words, try communicating through a video. After children feel comfortable having video equipment around (so they no longer notice its presence), record children demon-strating problem-solving skills as they substitute objects for missing props, or social skills as they cooperate in various roles. Show the video at a parent meeting and point out the skills at work.

■ **Out of the Mouths of Babes.** Invite older preschoolers to dictate stories about a dramatic-play theme. This activity helps children practice summarizing events and highlights the link between speaking, writing, and reading. It also shows that you think dramatic play is an important activity. Share children's stories with parents and other family members.

■ **Accentuate the Positive.** As you review events of the day with a family member, don't forget dramatic play: "Peter played with José and Jenny in the housekeeping corner this morning. He's really learning the give and take of social situations. I wish you could have seen him share the props and many ideas for new roles."

■ **Share Written Observations.** Review anecdotal observations you make in the dramatic-play area with family members. Offer examples over a period of time that demonstrate how children's gains in dramatic-play skills also contribute to overall development.

■ **Encourage Dramatic Play at Home.** The send-home sheet at right is designed to help families increase their understanding of the value of dramatic play and the importance of letting children take the lead in developing play themes at home. (Permission is granted to duplicate other pages in the book which may benefit your families.)

LEARNING THROUGH DRAMATIC PLAY:
A MESSAGE TO PARENTS

Dear Parents,

One of the most popular places in our room is the dramatic-play area, because it's the setting for so many exciting dramas! Pretend families cook and eat there. Babies are cared for and loved. And you never know when courageous firefighters may come to everyone's rescue. Occasionally, to encourage new play themes, we transform the area into a restaurant, a store, an airport, even a spaceship, depending on children's interests.

You can help make your child's at-home dramatic play richer and more enjoyable by keeping these suggestions in mind:

1. Let your child take the lead in deciding what to play and what props are needed. Creativity, language, and problem-solving skills are all at work when your child develops a play theme, explains it to you, and finds materials to use as costumes and props. Encourage your child to take creative control with questions like, "What shall we play?" "What will we need?" "What role should I play?" If you are not sure what to do, ask, "What is my job?"

2. Let your child try his or her own solutions to problems, even if you think they will fail. Solving problems requires a flexible mind, and often, the will to try idea after idea until one finally works. Showing your child the solution will not be as meaningful as letting him or her figure it out.

3. Try not to stereotype play. Dramatic play is an opportunity for children to try on the many roles they observe in real life. Boys may want to play daddy or even mommy to a baby doll, and girls may want to be a construction worker building a giant tower. If children sense your displeasure, they may become less creative and gain less from the experience.

4. If weapon play troubles you, help your child find other ways to feel powerful and in control. Even when children aren't allowed to play with toy weapons, they may fashion weapon-like objects from sticks, brooms, blocks — just about anything. While the sight of your child trying to zap a pretend foe can be disturbing, keep in mind that the weapon is a means for him or her to feel powerful and in control. Children may also shoot or attack during play when they can't think of anything else to do. Try brainstorming with your child to find other ways to deal with monsters or villains, perhaps by suggesting that the monster might be kept in tow by a stronger, friendlier character.

As you know, pretend play doesn't require elaborate props or play settings. Children are perfectly content raiding the pots-and-pans cupboard or dressing up in your old clothes. The bedroom floor is a fine place to hold a tea party, and the sandbox is the perfect spot for burying treasure!

Most importantly, dramatic play opens up worlds of wonder, daring, and joy for your child. Support those worlds — and welcome an invitation to visit them!

SETTING THE STAGE
FOR DRAMATIC PLAY

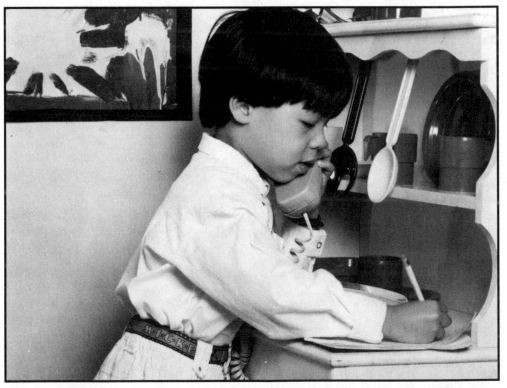

It's important to remember that young children's dramatic play really needs no stage, no agreed-upon place for making believe. Because pretending is a part of every young child's day, you'll find dramatic play wherever and whenever children use their imaginations to take on pretend roles.

Much of children's pretend play involves trying on the roles of parents, family members, and other important figures in their lives, as well as acting out situations they routinely take part in or see. Your housekeeping area can offer an exciting, inspirational setting.

Just as in all the other areas of your room, the attention and interest you show in the dramatic-play and/or housekeeping area communicates to children that you value this kind of play. The furnishings and props you provide and the way in which materials are organized

PHOTO: DIANA KASSIR

have a direct affect on the type and quality of play and the level of independence children feel as they create and become involved in their own themes and scenarios.

At the same time, stock other areas of your room with dramatic-play props so children might become construction workers in the block corner, sailors crossing the ocean at the water table, treasure hunters looking for gold in the sandbox, or whatever else they might choose.

This section will help you create a physical environment that is not only appropriate to the age and level of development of your children, but also encourages rich, imaginative, and satisfying play.

CREATING THE RIGHT SPACE

■ Consider the location.

Imagine that you are about to set up a dramatic-play area in your setting for the first time. Where would be the best location? Because you'll want children to feel free to talk and make sound effects as they take on various roles, you may want to position this area away from quieter areas, such as the book or cozy corners. At the same time, many dramatic-play themes are enhanced as they spill into other activity areas, such as the block corner or the location of gross-motor equipment like the climber or rocking boat. You'll want your dramatic-play and/or housekeeping area in a place where these materials can easily become extensions of dramatic play.

■ Plot out the space.

Look for ways to make this space visually different from the rest of your room. To encourage a variety of role-playing, you might separate the area into "rooms" by using various props to create small spaces — a kitchen, living room, and bedroom. Check the diagram on pages 30-31 for further guidance. Here are additional ideas for enhancing your dramatic-play area:

• Hang "kitcheny" wallpaper on one wall, starting about four feet above the floor, to establish a kitchen area.
• Use an area rug to mark a separate space, such as the living room. Make sure you tack the rug securely.
• Hang a pair of curtains on a wall to create the look of a bedroom or living room window. You might hang a poster of an outdoor scene behind the curtain. Change the poster from time to time, perhaps to reflect the current season. Or, suggest that children draw or paint their own scenes.
• Create "walls" to separate the rooms of the house. Strategically placed furniture, such as a set of shelves placed in the middle of the area, can give the affect of a wall separating a living room from a bedroom. A cloth curtain hung from a rod suspended from the ceiling can separate play areas.

■ Furnish your "home."
With the physical space defined, you can begin adding props and furnishings. Remember, the items you include will influence the type of situations children act out. Try these.

Child-sized basics:
  • stove
  • sink
  • refrigerator
  • table and chairs
  • doll bed or baby crib
  • full-length, unbreakable mirror
  • shelves

Kitchen equipment plays an important role in your area because it allows children to role-play a variety of familiar routines and events such as preparing meals, eating at a restaurant, inviting a teddy bear to tea, etc. In many homes, the kitchen table is a gathering spot for many activities beyond eating, so be sure children can move the table and chairs around themselves to accommodate their play.

Shelves well within children's reach are a practical addition. You'll need at least one set for storing kitchen props

and perhaps another near the mirror to store shoes, purses, and other dress-up accessories. You may also want to provide hampers, crates, a chest — any receptacles to make cleanup quicker, easier, and more organized.

Naturally, if your space and budget allow, there are many other pieces of furniture and large props that will encourage play:

- soft "living room" furniture
- closets
- an ironing board
- doll bunk beds and cradles
- doll strollers
- doll high chairs
- a washing machine

You may be able improvise some of these items, such as the closets and washing machine, using large cardboard boxes. Involve children in deciding what boxes can become and in dec-

orating and adding details. By observing while children play, you'll be able to pick up on their needs and interests — and together create from there.

CHOOSING PROPS AND ACCESSORIES

The richness of children's play will depend not only on basic furnishings and children's imaginations, but also on accessory objects. However, there is a fine line between giving children everything they need and allowing them to plan, gather, and improvise — to use their own creative abilities.

With young children who depend heavily on props to direct their play themes, you may want to guide play by providing a few well-chosen, realistic props. With older ones who may plan out their play and more readily substi-

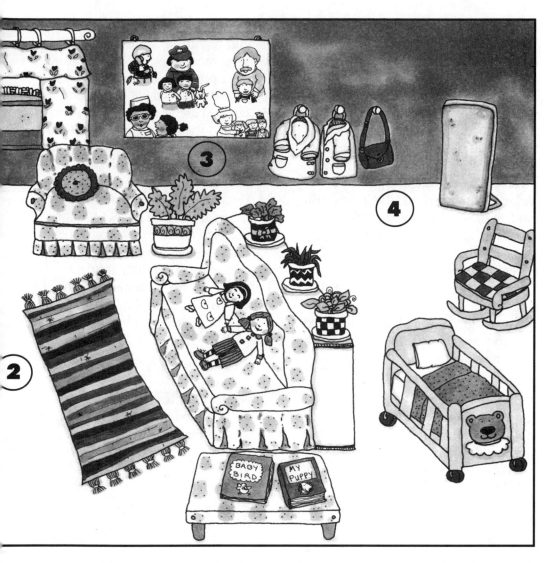

AN IDEAL SET-UP

The illustration at left shows a dramatic-play area based on a home environment, but adaptable to many themes. (Situating your dramatic-play area near your block corner will enable children to expand their play in all sorts of creative ways.) The numbers in the illustration coincide with the suggestions below. Please refer to "Setting the Stage," pages 28–34, for more detailed guidelines.

1. Define a kitchen area and stock it with various empty and clean food containers that children might find in their homes. Also include unbreakable pots, pans, dishes, and other kitchen-type, child-safe props. Make sure tables and chairs are easy for children to move as their play themes change.

2. A living-room area provides a cozy place for pretend play. Props can include safe items children might find in their homes, such as magazines, dolls to represent family members, and various pieces of comfortable furniture.

3. Pictures on the walls should be at children's eye level. Try using ones created by your children, such as a group collage of the various people who are important in their lives.

4. Provide a space where children can put on dress-up clothes and view themselves (in an unbreakable mirror). If possible, offer many kinds of clothes, as well as scarves, capes, and other nongender items, to inspire imaginative play.

tute one object — even a fairly abstract one — for another, you'll want to fuel their creative abilities. If older children are interested in a particular theme, you might encourage them to brainstorm props they'll need: "What do we need to make a restaurant?" "What could you use for a cash register?" Let the children take the lead. Don't feel compelled to fill in all the items. Simply step back and let the play grow as children's ideas develop.

When children tire of a particular play theme, consider storing special play props in labeled "prop boxes." You can bring these out again at a later time, perhaps to use with a different group of children.

Remember, for a child of any age, there can be too many props and toys. When you observe that children are spending more time manipulating ob-

jects than using those objects in pretend roles, it's time to simplify the dramatic-play area by putting some materials away. Stimulate new ideas for play by sharing a wonderful book, taking a field trip, or simply starting an open-ended discussion at circle time.

PROPS AND TIPS

■ **Dolls –** Dolls and doll clothes are important basic props. Keep in mind that children need to see themselves and their families reflected in their environment, so you'll need dolls of different genders, ages, races, and ethnicities — ideally, at least two dolls of each race/ethnicity, one male and one female. Also, try to provide dolls with disabilities and some of the aids they use — a doll in a wheelchair or a brace, or a doll who uses Braille or a hearing aid.

DEVELOPMENTAL CONSIDERATIONS

■ **Start simple.** Twos, younger threes, special-needs children, and any children who are inexperienced in dramatic play can be overwhelmed by too many furnishings and props. Focus on familiar settings by sticking to basic equipment and a few well-chosen, realistic props. A house and car are ideal settings for this group.

Realistic props are very important because, at this stage, the prop itself usually suggests the play theme. As children become more skilled at pretending, add other familiar props such as empty, clean milk cartons, cereal boxes, juice containers, and other items children routinely see and handle that might suggest a store.

■ **Provide the means for more complex play.** Children of any age who have engaged in a lot of dramatic play are ready for a wider range of settings and play themes. With older preschoolers, your challenge is to offer a variety of props and the basic framework for a setting.

As children progress in their dramatic play, don't shy away from props that are more abstract. For

Sharing dolls with another group is one way to increase the diversity of your own collection.

Doll-Play Tips:
• Keep dolls in good condition. Have an occasional bath day when everyone who is interested gets involved. In warm weather, try doing this outside.
• Keep doll clothes in good repair. Velcro fasteners and elastic on doll clothes make it easier for children to dress and undress their dolls. Repair rips, tears, and loose buttons you discover immediately.
• Have a special place to keep doll clothes.
• Provide lots of doll blankets. Children love to wrap babies in blankets or tuck them in at night.

■ **Household Props** – Dishes, pots and pans, play food — all of the items that are part of everyday life can be part of your housekeeping corner. Add objects from home for variety and realism, provided they pass safety inspection. (Toy-supply catalogs also carry a wealth of materials for the dramatic-play center. And many items you can easily make yourself.)

Here's a list of possible materials for different "rooms":
• Bedroom: sheets, blankets, and pillows for doll beds; a teddy bear; a child-sized rocking chair
• Living Room: books, newspapers, magazines, and a telephone
• Kitchen: pots and pans; wooden spoons; plastic silverware and dishes; placemats and napkins; potholders, dishcloths, and towels; dish drainers; empty food boxes and washed cans; and food made of nontoxic plastic or clay.

Household-Play Hints:
• Display photos in or near your housekeeping area that show families of many different racial and ethnic backgrounds and family configurations (single parent with children, an extended family, etc.) involved in a variety of

household activities such as cooking, cleaning, repairing items, reading, or playing games together. Also feature pictures of people with various disabilities doing work in and out of the home.
• Encourage parents to save empty containers from special ethnic foods, such as food boxes and cans written in Spanish or Arabic, to add diversity and realism.
• Make simple one-dimensional foods for children to serve on plates by cutting out color pictures of foods from magazines and laminating or covering with clear contact paper for durability.
• Let children bring water into their kitchen to expand the activities. Children can use it to wash dishes, dolls, doll clothes, or use the water in their "cooking."

■ **Dress-up Clothes** – Clothing props are so much a part of pretending. Provide an assortment of male and female clothing items, as well as extras such as purses and shopping bags, wallets, and eyeglass frames and cases. Remember, for health reasons hats should be washable, preferably plastic, and all clothing and props should be cleaned regularly.

Tips for Dress-up Play:
• Rotate dress-up clothes to encourage different roles.
• Provide items of modern clothing worn by people of different ethnic groups. (Consult families in your program.) Help older children understand the difference between everyday clothing and traditional or ceremonial clothing, and when and why the latter would be worn.
• Shorten dresses by cutting a few inches off the hem so they don't drag on the floor and cause children to trip. Replace difficult fasteners with ones children can manipulate easily, such as Velcro.
• Have an occasional "wash day" and invite children to help.
• Include a variety of large fabric pieces that children can fashion in their own ways to use for capes, head coverings, doll blankets, tablecloths, etc.

■ **Job-Specific Items** – Children like to play out the roles of adults they view as important. Parents can be very helpful in donating work-oriented props or materials they no longer need from their workplaces, such as briefcases, lunchboxes, clipboards, special work shirts, earphones, child-safe tool kits, aprons, food trays, tickets, brochures, etc.

"Career-Play" Tips:

• Inspect each item donated to insure that it's safe for children to use. Look for sharp edges and small parts that could be swallowed. Discard anything, no matter how appealing, that could be a safety hazard.

• To enhance and inspire play themes, post pictures at children's eye level of men and women of different races, ethnicities, and abilities engaged in many different professions.

• Display books on various jobs for children to look at when interested.

• If possible, as a group, visit parents' and other family members' workplaces, and/or invite family members to tell about their work and bring photographs to share.

• Remember that it is the children who are directors and inventors of their play. Props are merely tools to help children carry out and expand their ideas.

FINDING A PLACE FOR EVERYTHING

A certain amount of disorder is inevitable in every dramatic-play area, so it's important to organize materials so that children can easily get what they want without having to pull out what they don't want. By identifying a special place for everything, cleanup becomes that much easier.

■ Hang clothes on racks or hooks. When dress-up clothes are stored in a box or trunk, children must throw out everything to find what they want, creating instant disorder. Attach a mug rack to a wall or to the back of a shelf at children's height for hanging up dress-up clothes and sew loops in clothes so that children can easily hang them up.

■ Use shelves to hold more than books. Designate shelf space for shoes, purses, and other dress-up accessories. Small pictures of these items glued to the shelves will remind children what belongs where. Organize small, loose objects in clear plastic boxes for storing on shelves. Picture labels on shelves give each box a designated spot.

■ Use ready-made organizers like shoebags and silverware trays. A shoebag on a wall at children's height can hold any number of objects that will fit inside its pockets, from small dolls to shoes. A drawer organizer can hold plastic silverware or small cooking utensils.

■ Hang a pegboard in the kitchen. Now you've got the start of an idea that turns cleanup into a shape-matching game. Trace the shape of each kitchen tool on colored contact paper. Cut out each shape and adhere it to the pegboard, inserting a hook above each. At cleanup time, children match shapes to utensils, then hang them on their pegboard hooks. (Attach a loop of string for hanging utensils without holes.) Utensils are easy to find and fun to put away. (Paper silhouettes can be glued to shelves for dishes and many other play props.)

DRAMATIC PLAY IS EVERYWHERE!

Dramatic play is more satisfying when children's play scenarios expand from the house area to other areas of your room. Sometimes this may happen quite naturally, but you can also encourage exciting pretend play in every area by providing well-chosen props and accessories. Here are ways to inspire additional dramatic play.

■ **The Block Corner** Foster pretend play in the block corner by providing props to wear, such as hard hats and police and firefighter hats. As you pick up on children's interests, subtle suggestions can encourage them to use blocks to build objects they can use in play scenarios — vehicles, beds, a corral or

instance, sections of garden hose, pieces of disassembled machinery, large plastic crates, and oddly shaped plastic foam blocks may suggest things to children you never thought of, inspire new themes as they interact with one another, and help them feel free to let their imaginations soar!

■ **Always think safety.** Because you may be providing children with items that were not designed as toys, examine each for potential hazards. Make sure any buttons are sewn on securely, and that there are no other loose, small objects on which children could choke. Check for tools and utensils with sharp edges.

■ **Observe, observe, observe.** We may mistakenly believe that since older preschoolers are more comfortable with engaging in dramatic play, they require less of our attention and observation. Not at all. To keep the quality of play as high as it has the potential to be, you need to watch and listen to children as they interact. Their interactions provide clues — what you might set out to fuel children's interests, or which new props you might offer to suggest new settings and stimulate imaginations.

ENGAGING BOYS AS WELL AS GIRLS

Evaluate your dramatic-play center. What kinds of themes are the props most likely to encourage? Will both boys and girls be attracted to this area? Sometimes enticing boys to play in and "use" the house area can be a challenge, so consider expanding your dramatic-play area. These ideas will help stimulate diverse kinds of play.

■ Include a "fix-it and make-it" table equipped with toy tools, paste, wood, a paintbrush, and gardening tools.

■ Set up a table or desk and a variety of writing tools — a working typewriter, an adding machine, paper, pencils, paper clips, and a telephone. (This office-type environment will inspire many kinds of play as well as encourage early literacy skills.)

■ From time to time, transform the house area into a hospital, factory, or restaurant. Take your cues from children's interests and experiences, then tailor your basic furnishings and props to enhance them. Items such as the stove, sink, and refrigerator can become the kitchen where food for the workers or customers is prepared. Add other furniture such as tables and chairs or a small sofa. Feature props used by all kinds of workers.

cage for animals, even a house to climb inside. Most importantly, make sure children feel free to move items from one area of the room to another.

When children manipulate small figures — vehicles, animals, and people — this is also dramatic play. However, instead of playing a role themselves, children are using objects as symbols. They may have created a building or enclosure and extended their pretend world by playing several roles simultaneously — manipulating different dolls and props. To encourage this type of play, include small figures of people and furniture, as well as cars, trucks, and animals. (For more ideas, see Scholastic's activity book *Learning Through Play: Blocks*.)

■ **Puppet Play** – When children interact with puppets and make them talk and interact with one another, they are also involved in dramatic play. This type of play is excellent for developing language and for expressing feelings.

Have an interesting variety of puppets for children to use. (Make sure puppets are small enough for children to manipulate easily.) Rather than encouraging children to use puppets as characters in a memorized skit, you might put a puppet on your hand and ask it open-ended questions such as, "Hi, Whiskers, how are you feeling today? What would you like to tell me about?" Whiskers might then tell you about his new baby brother, his mom's business trip, his favorite toy, or any subject that is relevant to the children in your group.

As you engage in a conversation, encourage children to join in. Whiskers might ask children open-ended questions or be the main character in a story you make up together. Leave Whiskers and "his friends" out so children can play with puppets any time they'd like.

A stage can inspire imaginative play and performances. You can use a cardboard box or turn a table on its side. As with puppets, rather than direct children's actions or expect them to memo-

rize lines, encourage small groups of older preschoolers to improvise a familiar story, such as "The Three Bears," or create their own story while you help narrate.

■ **Sand and Water Table** – Small boats or objects that can serve as rafts and various figures of people are among the objects that will inspire symbolic pretend play at the water table. At the sand table, small people, animals, creatures like dinosaurs, and small cars and trucks can inspire dramatic-play themes. All children need is time to get involved.

■ **On the Playground** – As you know, children often enjoy engaging in dramatic play in outdoor settings. Open spaces of the playground expand the possibilities for dramatic-play themes. Riding toys may inspire drive-in restaurants, drive-through banks, or police and traffic play. Jungle gyms can become castle towers or caves.

Equipment on the playground also encourages dramatic play. The climber can make a great ship's mast or a mountaintop. Props such as small flags, tubes to look through, and megaphones can help children develop these and other themes. Many playgrounds have small playhouses that can be the setting for many different activities. Let children add furniture, signs, and other props. (Many commercially made child-sized storefronts are sturdy enough for outdoor use.)

Encourage outdoor dramatic play by taking large vinyl-covered blocks outside. Fill boxes with old pots and pans for cooking with dirt or sand, small figures for symbolic dramatic play, hats, and other durable, easy-to-clean props. To help keep track of the props, list the contents on the side of the box. At cleanup time, help children return the props by checking the lists together.

Karen Miller, special projects editor for *Pre-K Today,* is the author of a number of books for early childhood professionals including Scholastic's activity book *Learning Through Play: Blocks.*

ACTIVITY PLANS
FOR TWOS, THREES, FOURS, AND FIVES

USING THE
ACTIVITY PLANS

Pretend play is an important, exciting part of childhood and can take place in any or all areas of your setting throughout the day. When left to their own imaginations, children create all kinds of wonderful scenarios. They design settings, gather props, assign roles, and direct the play in their own ways.

Yet there are times when children need a spark to ignite their creative energy. There may be times when your dramatic-play area seems less popular. Or you may be looking for ways to help children incorporate more of their own experiences into their dramatic play. The activity plans that follow offer ways to expand on topics of natural interest to children, while still letting children take the lead in deciding how to use the materials and what roles to play. *Designed for children ages two to five, these activities are not intended to replace their own creative play.* Rather, they are designed to enhance it with themes and ideas that are appropriate to each age's developmental abilities and interests. Keep the plans in an accessible place, and pull them out as they relate to topics that come from your group. Consider them as starting points, building blocks, or idea resources to help you tailor your curriculum to children's interests and experiences.

These 40 child-centered plans encourage children to explore concepts and ideas. At the same time, they enable children to use dramatic play as it's meant to be used — as an avenue for expressing ideas and feelings, trying out the roles of significant persons in their own lives, experimenting with power, and expanding and enriching their already vivid imaginations!

UNDERSTANDING YOUR ROLE

Because children's dramatic-play themes should be allowed to come from their own thoughts and ideas, the plans have been designed to require a minimum of teacher involvement and direction. By taking your cues from the children in your group, you can provide related materials and props, and then step back and quietly observe. This gives children the creative freedom they need to experiment with roles, add new props, make decisions, and solve problems on their own.

As children play, look for appropriate times — generally moments when you won't interrupt play — to step into the play by assuming a role that can enhance the play, and then step out; to introduce a new prop that may spur ideas; or to assist children with particularly stubborn problems. Think of yourself as an assistant who knows that children have the leading roles in all their dramas, yet who is there to support the players and help insure that their play will be fulfilling.

GETTING THE MOST OUT OF THE ACTIVITY PLANS

The plans have been written and designed for children ages two to five, but remember, these ages represent a wide range of developmental levels. You may find that certain plans need to be adapted to meet the particular needs and interests of your group. The key is to be aware of your children's developmental levels and to look for ways to enhance *their* interests and experiences with appropriate activities.

The format is simple and easy to follow. Each plan includes most of these sections:

■ *Aim*: The value of the activity is outlined through a listing of the learning and developmental areas that will be tapped.

■ *Group Size*: The suggested group size is the optimum number of children to involve at a time. Naturally, you can adjust this number to meet your needs.

■ *Materials*: Props or materials for creating settings are suggested here. You may find you'll want or need to add or subtract items from this list based on your children's interests or on your own resources.

■ *In Advance*: This is an occasional heading found in some plans. It may suggest props to make before introducing a theme, or ideas for enlisting family or community members in donating materials.

■ *Set the Stage*: This is another occasional heading found in some plans. It outlines ways to ease children into a play theme, giving you time to observe their familiarity with the theme and/or the kinds of spontaneous dramas they may develop.

■ *Getting Ready*: Here you'll find suggested ways to introduce the theme to a large group at circle time or to a small group. Open-ended questions help children think about a topic and help you find out their familiarity with it. Brainstorming ideas, creating experience charts, taking field trips, or reading recommended stories are other ways to encourage involvement. Or simply set out props in the dramatic-play area without saying anything and then observe as play develops.

■ *Begin*: This is the "how to" section of the activity. Suggestions for expanding on evolving play themes, for organizing materials, and for involving children are included with each plan. Open-ended questions offer ways to stimulate children to come up with new ideas without imposing your own. As you introduce and supervise each activity, let children have plenty of time to explore and experiment with the theme. If a grocery store turns into a movie theater, that's okay.

■ *Remember*: This section offers developmental considerations to keep in mind when planning the activity. You may also find safety tips and suggested ways to expand on a particular theme or concept.

■ *Books*: The books listed at the bottom of each page have been carefully selected to reinforce the dramatic-play theme. They can be read before the activity as a way to introduce the theme and to inspire roles or props, or after, to follow up and perhaps close an activity.

SHARING THE PLANS WITH OTHERS

To get the most out of the activity plans featured in this guide, consider making them available to assistant teachers, aides, volunteers, and family members. (You have permission to duplicate all activity pages for educational use.)

When you share these plans, you communicate your philosophy of child-centered teaching to others. By offering tips on how to plan and organize activities, you help other adults interact with young children in ways that let children take the lead in creating their own worlds of make-believe.

USING THE ACTIVITY INDEX

The index on pages 78-79 lists each activity plan, along with the developmental areas and skills it enhances. Use the index to:

■ Determine the range of developmental areas covered in the plans.

■ Highlight specific skills a plan reinforces when talking to family members.

■ Identify and locate activity plans that reinforce particular skills on which you want to focus.

■ Assist you in finding themes that pick up on your group's present interest.

DRAMATIC PLAY

Twos enjoy acting out the familiar routines of their day.

THIS IS MY DAY

Aim: Children will use dramatic-play, language, and sequencing skills.

Group Size: Two or three children.

Materials: Blankets, stuffed animals, pretend groceries, kitchen utensils, child-sized tables and chairs, dolls, picture books, and other dramatic-play props; and pictures of people engaged in daily routines such as waking up, shopping, cooking, and going to bed.

GETTING READY

At circle time, share the pictures you've collected. Encourage children to name the activities and describe what the people are doing. Invite children to share their own experiences by commenting on the pictures and asking open-ended questions such as, "Yes, the boy is eating cereal. What do you like to eat for breakfast?"

After your discussion, end with this action song to the tune of "Here We Go 'Round the Mulberry Bush." Pantomime these routines as you sing together:

> *This is the way we rise and shine,*
> *Rise and shine, rise and shine.*
> *This is the way we rise and shine*
> *So early in the morning.*

(Repeat, substituting *wash our faces*, *brush our teeth*, *eat our breakfast*, *put on our clothes*, etc.)

BEGIN

Start by saying, "Let's play a pretending game. First we'll pretend we're sleeping. Then we'll pretend that we're waking up and doing some of the things you do at home before you come here each day."

Help the children set the scene. They can use blocks to make "beds" or spread blankets on the floor. Invite them to choose a stuffed animal or doll to take to bed with them, and get one for yourself.

When everyone is "sleeping," you might say: "Listen! The birds are singing. The sun is coming up. Let's pretend we're waking up. Show me how you wake up." Give children time to think, and encourage them to pretend in their own ways. Join in when children are engaged in pretending, so they don't just copy your actions.

Guide children into another routine by asking them what they do next: "After you get up, what do you do? Do you wash your

face? Do you eat breakfast first?" As children pretend, comment on individual differences: "I see Joshua gets out of bed quickly. I like to wake up slowly. Keisha gets dressed before breakfast. Melanie gets dressed after she eats."

Continue acting out other parts of the day. For each activity, ask open-ended questions to help children think ahead: "How do you get to school?" "What do we do first?" At "bedtime," review the events of this "day." You might finish by reading a "goodnight" story aloud.

Remember

▪ Understanding the sequence of the day helps twos develop a sense of continuity between home and school, which can help them feel more secure in your program.

▪ Young twos with short attention spans may be more comfortable acting out only one routine each day.

▪ You might try some of these ideas while children are playing house to enrich their play.

▪ Everyone's daily routine is different. Accept each child's contributions as you encourage everyone to participate.

BOOKS

Share these books about daily happenings.

▪ *The First Words Picture Book* by Bill Gillham (Coward, McCann & Geoghegan)

▪ *How Do I Put It On?* by Shigeo Watanabe (Putnam Publishing Group)

▪ *Ten, Nine, Eight* by Molly Bang (Greenwillow Books)

DRAMATIC PLAY

Your twos will love using playdough as pretend cooks and bakers.

FUN WITH PLAY CLAY!

Aim: Children will develop skills in symbolic play, social interaction, language, and fine-motor control.

Group Size: One to five children.

Materials: Commercial or homemade playdough; an assortment of plastic lids and tops; nested measuring cups; wide and narrow wooden craft sticks (or clean ice cream sticks and tongue depressors); and clay boards (optional).

In Advance: If desired, make clay boards by covering both sides of one-foot-square pieces of Masonite with high-gloss, easy-to-wash paint.

GETTING READY

Set up a place for each child with a large mound of playdough, a few lids or tops, at least one measuring cup, and a few craft sticks.

BEGIN

Cooking, serving, and eating are favorite pretend themes for twos. Let children play freely with the playdough. Many will spontaneously begin to make "food," turning the containers into cooking pots or dishes and using the sticks for cutting and serving. Along with countless cups of coffee, you may be invited to taste everything from "soup" to "ice cream cones," offering wonderful opportunities for you to help expand and enrich this use of language and imagination.

For example, if Donna announces, "I'm making cookies," follow along with her theme by responding, "They smell delicious! What kind are they?" If she responds, "chocolate chip," you might pretend to sample her cookies. Extend the play by asking, "I love cookies! Do you have any other kinds?" If she needs help responding to this question, invite her to choose an answer: "Do you have peanut butter or oatmeal cookies?"

Be creative and playful in responding to children's play themes. Being offered a simple cup of coffee, for example, can lead play in interesting directions if you pretend it is too hot or in need of sugar. When shown a "birthday cake," you might suggest a chorus of "Happy Birthday," then pretend to blow out the candles. Be sure to inquire about the flavor of the cake, frosting, and ice cream.

Remember

▪ Young twos often respond to humorous dramatic exaggeration, such as watching you gobble up food like "Cookie Monster."
▪ To ensure the safety of this activity, check that there are no rough edges on the plastic items and that all wood is splinterproof.

BOOKS

| Share these books about cooking and eating with twos. | ▪ *Let's Eat* by True Kelly (E.P. Dutton) | ▪ *Max's Chocolate Chicken* by Rosemary Wells (Dial Books) | ▪ *My Kitchen* by Harlow Rockwell (Greenwillow Books) |

DRAMATIC PLAY

Pretending with the telephone can help children cope with separation.

WHO'S ON THE TELEPHONE?

Aim: Children use dramatic-play and language skills while exploring feelings associated with separation.

Group Size: One to three children.

Materials: Several toy telephones; and props associated with family members' non-home activities, such as purses, briefcases, lunchboxes, suitcases, hats, and keys.

SET THE STAGE

Add the telephones and other props to your dramatic-play area (if they're not already there). Observe children's play for themes related to separation, such as family members leaving for work or calling a babysitter. (Remember that children are more likely to play the adult roles.) Watch for signs of separation anxiety — crying/asking for family members, withdrawal, aggression, and regression.

GETTING READY

When you observe that a child is missing family members, ask if he or she would like to make a pretend call to someone special. Make sure the child understands the call is make-believe. By gently helping the child to verbalize feelings, you may help to ease her anxiety.

BEGIN

Ask the child whom she would like to call. You might pretend to place the call yourself. Or "make" the phone ring, answer, then hand it to the child, saying, "It's for you. Who do you think it is?"

Take your cues from the child. Some will prefer that you do the talking. Try to involve the child by encouraging her to direct you: "Grandma's on the phone? What should I say to her?"

With some children you may need to carry the pretend conversation, pausing to let the child give you clues: "Hi, Jesse's mommy. How are you? I'm fine, thank you. Jesse is playing with the suitcase and packing all the clothes. Are you at work? Jesse misses you. We're going to write you a note when we hang up. What time will you pick Jesse up tonight? After snacktime? Okay, we'll see you then." Before you hang up, offer Jesse a chance to talk. If she'd rather not, you might ask, "Shall we call someone else, or would you like to write a note to Mommy now?"

Remember

▪ Through activities like these, even reluctant children may begin to make pretend calls to loved ones.

▪ Very young children may not be able to express feelings directly. Encourage telephone play by focusing on dolls or animals. You might say, "Oh, Baby Bunny is crying. I think she misses her family. Shall we call them? Whom shall we call? Her daddy? Do you want to call? What should we say to her daddy?"

▪ Ask family members to write notes to children to keep in their cubbies. Also display photos of children and their families. Then when a child is sad, read the note and talk about the family picture together.

▪ Many twos need a security object — a blanket or stuffed animal — to hold during times of stress. Suggest that children store these in cubbies or on a special shelf.

BOOKS

Share these books that have separation themes with twos.

▪ *Goodbye House* by Frank Asch (Prentice-Hall)

▪ *Where Are You Going, Emma?* by Jeanne Titherington (Greenwillow Books)

▪ *Anna's Secret Friend* by Yoriko Tsutsui (Viking Kestral)

DRAMATIC PLAY

Your twos will feel "big" when it's their turn to put babies to sleep.

TAKING CARE OF BABIES

Aim: Children will use dramatic-play, language, and fine-motor skills.

Group Size: Two or three children.

Materials: A baby doll for each child; baby beds; baby clothes and blankets; baby-care items such as diapers, plastic bottles, bibs, and rattles; and clean, empty plastic containers for baby powder, wipes, shampoo, and lotion.

In Advance: Ask families to lend spare baby items. Aim for an assortment of basics so that children will have props for different baby-care activities.

GETTING READY

Invite children to share the baby items they have brought from home. Ask questions to encourage them to talk about the items: "Eric, can you fit into that outfit anymore?" "Mariann, do you need to wear a bib now when we have a snack at school?"

BEGIN

Invite a few children to choose and care for a baby doll. Together look at the different baby items they can use. (To start, limit this selection to some basic items so children are not overwhelmed. Add more items as play develops.)

Let children create their own baby-caregiver scenarios. Most will immediately begin dressing, diapering, washing, or rocking. Take part only if the child seems truly unable to think of something to do. You might ask, "Is it time for your baby to go to bed? How can you get your baby to fall asleep? How does your mommy (daddy, grandma, aunt, etc.) help you go to sleep?" Or take a role in the play. Holding a baby doll, you might sit down next to another child and say, "My baby doesn't want to take a nap. What do you think I should do?"

Sing a Baby Song

Here's a song twos can sing to their babies to help them fall asleep. It's sung to the tune of "Row, Row, Row Your Boat."

> *Hush, hush, hush-a-bye.*
> *Sleep my little one.*
> *Hush, hush, hush-a-bye.*
> *Now the day is done.*

Remember

▪ Twos will also enjoy showing others items they used or wore when they were babies. However, some twos will not want to share the baby items they have brought from home. Rather than force a child to share, have plenty of other items from which to choose.

▪ Remind children not to put toy or real bottles in their mouths.

▪ Many twos have strong feelings about baby items they have given up or are trying to give up, such as bottles. Be sensitive to their feelings. Don't be surprised if they regress and start to play baby. This is usually temporary. Let children express their feelings, and assure them that it's okay to feel as they do.

BOOKS

Share these books about babies.

▪ *The Blanket* by John Burningham (Thomas Y. Crowell)

▪ *Max's Bedtime* by Rosemary Wells (Dial Books)

▪ *Take a Nap, Harry* by Mary Chalmers (Harper & Row)

DRAMATIC PLAY

Add water play to pretend play for a splash of fun!

BATHING BABY

Aim: Through this nurturing activity, twos will begin to think about the needs of others. They will also use language, fine-motor, and dramatic-play skills, and experiment with water-related science concepts.

Group Size: One or two children.

Materials: A washable doll, doll blanket, small washcloth, towel, floating soap, plastic cup, and plastic dishpan for each setup; a large towel to protect the surface under each dishpan.

In Advance: Fill the dishpans about one-third full of warm water, and set on a thick towel to absorb any splashed water. Place the soap, washcloth, and cup next to the pan, with a towel and blanket nearby.

GETTING READY

Read a story about babies, such as one listed below. Talk about things babies need. Invite children to use a doll to show how they would feed, carry, and comfort a baby. Then talk about bathing a baby. Ask, "Does your baby need a bath? How do you know? What will you need to give your baby a bath?"

BEGIN

Invite one or two interested children at a time to use the materials you have set up. Then step back and observe. Prompt now and then with questions to keep the play going: "Does your baby's hair need to be washed? How could you rinse out the soap?" or "How could you dry off your baby? What can you use to keep your baby warm?"

Watch for the different ways in which twos try to care for their babies. They are demonstrating a beginning understanding of the needs of others. Reinforce their actions by commenting on how well they care for their babies.

Sing a Bathtime Song

Sing this song with twos while they bathe their babies. The tune is "Skip to My Lou."

> *Wash, wash, wash my baby.*
> *Wash, wash, wash my baby.*
> *Wash, wash, wash my baby.*
> *Wash my darling baby.*

Continue with other verses: *rinse, rinse, rinse* and *dry, dry, dry*.

Remember

▪ Be sure to have extra setups on hand for children who can't wait for a turn. Children should be free to take as long as they want with this relaxing activity.

▪ Twos often play that soap gets in baby's eyes, which is their way of acting out an unpleasant bathtime experience. Acknowledge these feelings and encourage children to share them.

▪ This activity may trigger sharing of times when a child's baby sibling is given a bath at home. Encourage twos to share their feelings about siblings, and don't be surprised if baby doll gets an extra dose of soap in its eyes.

BOOKS

Share these books about babies.

▪ *Betsy and Peter Are Different* by Gunilla Wolde (Random House)

▪ *My Baby Brother Needs a Friend* by Jane Belk Moncure (Child's World)

▪ *Babies* by Rachel Isadora (Greenwillow Books)

DRAMATIC PLAY

Twos can use dolls to act out feelings associated with this common experience.

GOING TO THE DOCTOR

Aim: Children will use dramatic-play, language, and fine-motor skills while developing an understanding of their own bodies and the role of an important community helper, the doctor.

Group Size: Two or three children.

Materials: Baby dolls; two or more doctor kits with an assortment of instruments; materials for bandages (strips of cloth or gauze and masking tape); doctor and nurse clothing; and a scale (optional).

GETTING READY

Invite children to share their own experiences with going to the doctor. It may be helpful to show them pictures of a doctor's office or illustrations from one of the books listed below to stimulate discussion.

BEGIN

Introduce the doctor-play props. Give children time to examine each one. Discuss the name of each item and what it's used for.

Now invite children to role-play using the doctor's equipment by asking, "What would happen if one of our dolls got sick? Where could we take the doll? Would you like to make a doctor's office?"

Once you've introduced the idea, step back and give children

plenty of time to develop themes in their own ways. They may want to use the dramatic-play area to set up an office, or they may just find a comfortable place on the floor where they can "examine" and take care of their sick babies.

Weigh the Baby

When interest seems to wane, introduce a new prop, such as a balance scale or even a standard bathroom scale. Twos will enjoy experimenting with the scale, watching the dolls go up and down or the needle move. This kind of experimentation is wonderful; however, don't expect the children to understand the concept of weighing.

Remember

▪ Some young children have strong feelings of anger or fear attached to the experience of going to the doctor. Let them share their feelings, and communicate by your openness that it's okay to feel angry or afraid. You might share your own feelings about being sick and going to the doctor.

▪ Because twos may use doctor play to work out strong feelings, play can become aggressive. For this reason, limit "patients" to dolls or stuffed animals.

BOOKS

Share these books about going to the doctor.

▪ *My Doctor* by Harlow Rockwell (Macmillan)

▪ *Tommy Goes to the Doctor* by Gunilla Wolde (Houghton Mifflin)

▪ *Come to the Doctor, Harry* by Mary Chalmers (Harper & Row)

DRAMATIC PLAY

Washing dishes can be a treat for twos!

WASHING THE DISHES

Aim: Children will use dramatic-play, language, and fine-motor skills while also exploring science concepts related to water and bubbles.

Group Size: One or two children.

Materials: Plastic dishpans (have some in reserve); dish soap; sponges, dishcloths, and dish-cleaning brushes; a dish-drying rack; dish towels; larger towels to protect the surface under the pans; unbreakable plastic dishes and silverware to wash; and water-play smocks.

In Advance: Fill one or more dishpans one-third full with warm, sudsy water. Place thick towels under the pans to absorb splashes. Organize the play area so that twos can place the "dirty" dishes on one side of the pan and the "clean" dishes on the other. Dried dishes can go on another table or in the dish cupboard in your dramatic-play area.

GETTING READY

Introduce the theme of doing dishes by reading one of the books listed below or by talking about doing dishes at home. Ask, "Who does dishes in your house? Do you help sometimes? What do you need to wash dishes?" Encourage children to share their experiences with this familiar activity.

BEGIN

Show the dish-washing area you have set up to one or two interested children at a time. Then say: "Some of our play dishes really need washing. Would you like to wash some of them? Why don't you get the dishes you want to wash and bring them here."

Help children put on the smocks and get started. Then step back and observe. Give children plenty of time and freedom to explore the fun of washing dishes in their own ways. Some may wash the same dish over and over, while others will play with the soap suds and sponges. Experimenting with water and bubbles helps children learn the properties of these elements and, at the same time, enjoy a tactile experience.

Children may also expand their play to washing table tops and furniture. Be clear about what is not allowed (such as dumping water on the floor), but within these boundaries, let children develop their own play themes and activities.

Sing a Work Song

Sing this song with twos as they play. It's sung to the tune of "Frere Jacques."

Wash the dishes, wash the dishes.
Scrub, scrub, scrub.
Scrub, scrub, scrub.
Washing all the dishes, washing all the dishes
In the tub, in the tub.

Remember

- Most twos can't wait long for a turn. Have at least two extra setups ready to go.
- Bubbles are a great stimulus for language development. Listen for opportunities to expand vocabularies as children work.
- This kind of activity is often soothing for any child, especially one who is sad, angry, overly excited, or tense. You might consider setting up a dishpan in an area that is quiet and protected for a child who seems upset.

BOOKS

| Share these books with kitchen-activity themes. | ■ *A First Book in My Kitchen* by Zokeisha (Brimax) | ■ *Elsie Tidies Her House* by Anna Virin (Harvey House) | ■ *My Kitchen* by Harlow Rockwell (Greenwillow Books) |

DRAMATIC PLAY

Twos will enjoy caring for clothes, just like their family members do.

LAUNDRY DAY

Aim: Children will use dramatic-play, visual-discrimination, language, and fine-motor skills.

Group Size: Four to six children.

Materials: A laundry basket filled with clean clothes worn by various family members; doll clothes; several plastic dishpans; clothesline and clothespins; a toy iron and ironing board or table; plastic smocks; and towels to place under pans or clothesline.

In Advance: Fill each dishpan one-third full with warm, sudsy water. String the clothesline at children's height outdoors, if possible, and clip clothespins to it. (Lay towels or newspaper under an indoor line to catch drips.) Nearby, set up the iron and ironing board or table.

GETTING READY

At circle time, talk with children about doing laundry. Encourage them to relate their experiences at home or at a laundromat. Ask, "Who does the laundry in your family? Do you help? What part do you like best?"

Show children the laundry basket full of clothes. Pick up each item and ask, "What is this? Who might wear this?" Explain that these clothes are clean, but they need to be ironed. Ask, "What do you do when you iron? Who irons clothes at your house?" Remind children that they can iron at school because the iron is pretend and it does not get hot. Caution them *never* to touch a real iron at home.

BEGIN

Show a few children who are interested the dishpans and doll clothes that "need washing." Introduce others to the ironing area. Once children have started, step back and let their play develop. Talk with children about what they are doing. Discuss the suds in the washing water and where the bubbles come from. Comment on the job the ironers are doing.

When the washers start to tire, help them wring out the clothes. Then give them a container to carry the wet clothes to the clothesline to hang them up to dry.

Sing a Laundry-Day Song

As children work, sing this familiar song:

> *This is the way we wash our clothes,*
> *Wash our clothes, wash our clothes.*
> *This is the way we wash our clothes.*
> *So they look bright and shiny.*

Follow with other verses: *wring our clothes*; *hang up our clothes*; *iron our clothes*; and *fold our clothes*.

Remember

- Capitalize on the science opportunities in this activity. For example, as the clothes are drying, talk about the difference in the way the clothes feel when they are wet and dry.

- Twos love to match and sort. Include one clean sock from several clean sets in your laundry basket. Keep the matching socks in a paper bag. Give each child a sock to wear. Talk about the colors and patterns. Then, one at a time, pull a sock from the paper bag and ask twos to check if the sock matches the one they are wearing. Continue until each child is wearing matching socks.

BOOKS

Share these books about laundry days.	• *Baby's Sock* by Anne Baid (William Morrow & Co.)	• *Clothes* by Sara Lynn (Aladdin Books)	• *So Clean!* by Harriet Ziefert (Random House)

DRAMATIC PLAY

Involve twos in an activity they love — riding in the car!

LET'S GO FOR A DRIVE

Aim: Children will use dramatic-play, language, and motor skills.

Group Size: Two or three children.

Materials: Dolls, small chairs or hollow blocks to sit on, several steering wheels, a toy or real baby car seat, and an old car seat with a seat belt (optional).

GETTING READY

Introduce a discussion about riding in the car. (You might read one of the books listed below aloud.) Ask, "Where do you like to go in the car? Where do you sit? What do you see out the windows?"

BEGIN

Show children the steering wheels, dolls, and chairs or car seats. Ask, "What can you do with these? What can we pretend to play?" Give children time to play with the props in their own ways. Children may enjoy pretending to drive — putting the dolls in real or pretend car seats and going for a "spin." Some children may want to use blocks to make the shape of a car, but for most twos the fun is in pretending to drive.

Keep the play going or expand it by asking open-ended questions and assuming a role in the play: "John, where are you driving? May I ride with you? Could we pick up some groceries?" Or, "I wonder how many people can fit in this car for a ride?"

If your twos have ridden in a bus, they might like to pretend they are driving one. Arrange rows of chairs or blocks for seats and invite a large group of children to participate.

Sing a Driving Song

Riding in a car is a perfect time to sing a song. Try this variation on "Wheels on the Bus."

> *The wheels on the car go round and round,*
> *Round and round,*
> *Round and round.*
> *The wheels on the car go round and round,*
> *All through the town.*

Add other verses about the horn, windows, wipers, keys, and other parts of a vehicle.

Remember

▪ Check all real automobile parts to be sure there are no sharp edges or loose parts and they will be able to take rough play.

▪ Some urban children may have limited experience with riding in cars, but may be very familiar with buses, taxis, and subways or trains.

▪ Twos' language skills are rapidly increasing. As you interact during play, help them increase their vocabularies by using terms associated with vehicles and driving, such as *passenger*, *steering wheel*, *brakes*, *gas pedal*, *windshield wipers*, *engine*, *motor*, *tires*, *driver*, *headlights*, *seat belts*, etc.

BOOKS

| Share these books on cars with twos. | ▪ *When I Ride in a Car* by Dorothy Chlad (Children's Press) | ▪ *Cars* by Anne Rockwell (E.P. Dutton) | ▪ *Amy Loves the Rain* by Julia Hoban (Harper & Row) |

DRAMATIC PLAY

Turn your room into a mall and let twos imitate something adults do — shop!

THE SHOPPING TRIP

Aim: Children will use dramatic-play, math, language, and fine-motor skills.

Group Size: Two or three children.

Materials: Shopping bags and baskets or a toy shopping cart; wallets and purses; play money (optional); paper bags; items to purchase such as clothing, jewelry, toys, and food; and indoor riding toys, if available.

SET THE STAGE

Involve children in setting up areas of the room for shopping. You might set up signs for different stores — toys, food, etc. At each "store," display the wares on a table or on large blocks, and stock a few paper bags. Your dramatic-play area might be the home where shoppers leave from and return to.

GETTING READY

Describe a shopping trip you recently took. Ask your children if they have ever been shopping. What did they buy? Where did they go? Encourage children's use of language by prompting them to tell about how they get to shopping areas and with whom they go. Show pictures of all kinds of people shopping to help twos recall experiences to share.

BEGIN

Twos delight in putting little things inside of big things, so the shopping bags, baskets, and carts you provide will inspire your shoppers. Accompany the children on a walk to see the different shops. Encourage comments on the items in each store.

Next, take the group to the dramatic-play area and point out the wallets, purses, and shopping bags or baskets. This start is all they'll need, so step back and watch as they go to the stores to examine items, try them on, make purchases, and then take purchases home.

If available, indoor riding toys — or even outdoor toys brought in for this special activity — add a new dimension to play. Now children can drive to the stores, then drive home with their purchases.

Remember

▪ Young twos may be overwhelmed by too many shopping areas or by too many items in one area. Start simple (with one store), and add more as children seem ready.

▪ Older twos may enjoy putting up picture "signs" for each store or department. Enlist families to help collect magazine pictures of various items. Glue each set of pictures on oaktag, label, and cover with clear plastic. Twos will have fun matching signs to objects.

▪ Though you may plan this activity for a small group, others will want to join in. Try to have enough materials on hand for everyone to play a role.

▪ Because it is so mobile, this is an activity that can go on and on. If you see the same children in or near the same store all the time, don't interfere. Let them create the play they like best.

▪ Twos like being able to use a large space in their dramatic play, so allow plenty of room.

BOOKS

Share these books about shopping.

▪ *At the Stores* by Colin McNaughton (Philomel Books)

▪ *Shopping* by Sue Tarsky (Simon & Schuster)

▪ *The Shopping Basket* by John Burningham (Thomas Y. Crowell)

DRAMATIC PLAY

Try this familiar activity to help threes feel more comfortable and cozy.

MORNING AT MY HOUSE

Aim: Children will use dramatic-play and creative-thinking skills as well as their imaginations.

Group Size: Small or large group.

Materials: Empty cereal, milk, and juice containers; egg cartons; unbreakable cooking and eating utensils; children's clothing, such as slippers, pajamas, and robes; and bathroom props such as washcloths, towels, cardboard toothbrushes, combs, and brushes.

In Advance: Ask families to donate items such as those listed above for acting out morning routines. Be sure borrowed items that need to be returned are labeled with the child's name.

GETTING READY

Bring a small group of children together. Ask, "What do you do in the morning when you get up?" Give children time to share. Then, based on their responses, ask, "What's your favorite thing to do in the morning? What do you like to eat for breakfast?" (If children eat breakfast in your program, talk about what you eat and how you get ready to eat.) "Do you brush your own teeth? What do you need to brush your teeth?" As children relate their experiences, focus attention on similarities and differences: "Sam and Valerie have cereal for breakfast. Meg's big sister helps her get dressed. Yasmin's grandma walks her to school."

When children have had plenty of time to share, you might talk a little about your own morning routine — such as how and what you fix for breakfast, how you decide what to wear, what you do for other family members, and how you get to school.

BEGIN

Set out the props you've gathered, including those from families. Identify each item together, and talk about how each is used. Let children examine them. Then move all of the items to the dramatic-play area, and give children plenty of time to play.

Extending the Experience

Listen and observe as children play. Some children might like to share their thoughts and experiences by dictating a group experience story. Or children might like to help make breakfast at school and invite a family member to come to share it.

Remember

▪ Young threes' speech may consist of one-word responses or simple phrases. Help them develop language skills by expanding their responses into longer phrases and sentences.

▪ By providing children with opportunities to connect home and school, you can help ease anxieties stemming from separation. Help family members understand that discussions and dramatic-play activities based on familiar home routines can be comforting for children, especially as they work to make the transition from home to school. Listening to and observing children carefully can give you clues about how well individuals are adjusting.

▪ As you share information about your routines, remember that it can be difficult for threes to imagine you anywhere but in your program.

BOOKS

| Look for these books about morning routines. | ▪ *Is Anybody Up?* by Ellen Kandoian (Putnam Publishing Group) | ▪ *My Dressing Book* by Jane Gelbard and Betsy Bober Polivy (Grosset & Dunlap) | ▪ *Watch Me* by Anne Mazer (Alfred A. Knopf) |

DRAMATIC PLAY

Plan a special day. Invite threes' favorite toy friends.

FAVORITE TOY VISITING DAY

Aim: Children will develop dramatic-play, language, and social-interaction skills.

Group Size: Three or four children.

Materials: A stuffed animal or doll for each child, preferably one brought from home.

In Advance: A few days before "visiting day," send a note home requesting that families help their child choose a favorite stuffed animal or doll to bring on a particular day that week. If possible, bring in a treasured toy friend from your own childhood.

GETTING READY

On the day before visiting day, share your special toy. Explain why it's important to you, and let children gently touch and hold it. Then invite children to bring in a favorite toy friend of their own for a special visiting day.

As children arrive, make a name tag with the child's name and with the name of the toy friend. (Be sure to have some stuffed animals and dolls on hand for children to "adopt" for the day if they do not bring one from home.) Ask each child to introduce his or her special toy friend at circle time.

BEGIN

In small groups, invite children to reintroduce their special toy friends. Ask if anyone would like to pass around his or her toy for "hugs."

To encourage pretend play, language, and interaction, suggest children talk to one another's toy friends and have their "friends" converse with one another. (You can model this type of conversation with your own special toy.) Suggest children introduce the toys to dolls and stuffed animals in your dramatic-play or cozy area.

Let children include their toy friends in other activities during the day. For example, encourage them to make houses or furniture for their toys in the block area. Toy friends might watch water or sand play (from a safe distance), share a snack, or take a nap.

Remember
▪ Some children may want to play with certain other children and their visiting toys. You can help to organize these "play dates" during the day.

▪ Rather than ask threes to share their own toys, remind children to ask permission before touching or holding another child's toy. If this becomes a problem, clear off a high shelf where the visiting toys can rest safely when not in use.

BOOKS

| Share these books about special toys. | ▪ *Corduroy* by Don Freeman (Viking Penguin) | ▪ *The Friend* by John Burningham (Thomas Y. Crowell) | ▪ *William's Doll* by Charlotte Zolotow (Harper & Row) |

DRAMATIC PLAY

Invite threes to enjoy a familiar and favorite activity.

LET'S GO GROCERY SHOPPING!

Aim: Children will use dramatic-play and language skills as they begin to understand social studies concepts related to one kind of community helper.

Group Size: Two or three children.

Materials: Empty, clean food containers, such as cereal and cracker boxes, beverage cartons, plastic margarine containers, and catsup and mustard bottles; a grocer's apron; a cashier's smock; a toy cash register and play money; paper bags, purses, and baskets or toy shopping carts; a play telephone; and paper and markers.

GETTING READY

Encourage threes to share their experiences at a grocery store. Enhance the theme of shopping by sharing a book such as one listed below.

If possible, arrange for a group walk to a neighborhood grocery store. Call ahead to determine the best time to visit and whether someone will be available to answer children's questions. At the store, encourage children to identify foods they recognize. Discuss how foods of the same type are grouped together, such as fruits, vegetables, cereals, and canned foods, so that people can find them easily. Look at the labels that show how much items cost. Help children name the different people who work at a grocery store — the manager, cashiers, stock clerks, delivery people, etc. Discuss shopping routines such as getting shopping carts and paying for food. You might also check whether the store has items it could donate for props, such as plastic fruit baskets, sale signs, paper bags, or smocks with the store logo.

BEGIN

When you return, talk about the experience and ask if anyone would like to set up a grocery store near your dramatic-play area or in another spot. Offer children large blocks, plastic crates, or extra tables for store shelves or cashier's counters. Be sure to let children create the store according to their own design and ideas.

If necessary, discuss the different roles of customers and workers children might play. Then step back and let them develop the theme. Children will quite naturally begin to use the props and act out events they have experienced. Observe the play. At non-intrusive moments, you might comment on what they are doing: "Michael, I see you've bought a lot of food. Who will eat it?" "Charlene, would you like to work in the store? What would you like to do?"

Remember
▪ Children who are more action-oriented may want to take on the roles of people who deliver goods to the store or to customers.
▪ Some children may want to make signs for prices and sales by dictating to you or by scribbling their own pretend words and numbers.
▪ Children often enjoy making their own play money. Set out colored paper and child-safe scissors, and let them create their own shapes and amounts.

BOOKS
Share these books with a shopping theme.

▪ *Going Shopping* by Sarah Garland (Atlantic Monthly Press)

▪ *The Shopping Trip* by Helen Oxenbury (Dial Books)

▪ *The Supermarket Mice* by Margaret Gordon (E.P. Dutton)

DRAMATIC PLAY

Use this activity to turn your room into the best fishing hole in town!

GONE FISHING!

Aim: Children will develop science and social studies concepts while using eye-hand coordination and dramatic-play, creative-thinking, and problem-solving skills.

Group Size: Three to four children.

Materials: Large sheets of paper; blue, green, and white paint; sticks, dowels, or cardboard tubes; string; small magnets; large paper clips; staples; colored paper for making fish; scissors and crayons; and baskets, paper plates, or other containers in which to put fish.

GETTING READY

Gather together and ask children if they have ever been fishing or have ever seen anyone fish. Talk about all of the different places that people go to fish, such as oceans, ponds, lakes, rivers, and streams.

Encourage children to share their experiences. Then invite any who are interested to make a fishing pond (or lake, ocean, or river), fish to catch, and fishing rods so that they can turn a part of the room into a wonderful fishing area!

To make the pond, tape a large sheet of craft paper on the floor. Set out brushes and blue, green, and white paint. Talk about the colors of water and encourage children to cover the paper any way they would like.

Offer children colored paper, scissors, and crayons to make their own fish. Let them cut out fish in shapes and sizes they like and add features if they wish. Attach paper clips to large fish and

staples near the mouths of small fish. As you create your fish together, talk about fishing.

To make the fishing rods, tie magnets to one end of several lengths of string, and tie the strings to sticks, dowels, or cardboard tubes.

BEGIN

Invite an interested group of children to set up the pond in an area where it will be apart from other types of play. Encourage children to add details to the fishing area. For example, they could use large blocks or chairs to make boats or docks.

Leave children to play. If necessary, you might model how to "cast" out a line and catch a fish by getting the magnet close to a paper clip or staple. If play slows down, you might pretend to bait a hook or ask where the "best" fishing spot is. Threes might also have fun throwing fish they catch back into the pond, storing fish they catch in a basket, or setting up a fish market where they sell their fish to customers.

Remember

▪ Sticks or dowels can be dangerous for young threes. Keep them short and make sure there's enough room for children to "throw out" their lines without hitting others or getting their lines tangled up.

▪ Children may not want to share fish they've made and may also want to take them home. Cut out a variety of fish from paper or felt for everyone to use.

BOOKS

Share these books with your fishers.

▪ *The Berenstain Bears Go to Camp* by Stan and Jan Berenstain (Random House)

▪ *Fishes* by Brian Wildsmith (Franklin Watts)

▪ *The Little Fish That Got Away* by Bernadine Cook (Addison-Wesley)

DRAMATIC PLAY

Threes will enjoy pretending to plant and grow a magnificent garden!

SANDBOX GARDENING

Aim: Children will develop science and social studies concepts and use dramatic-play, creative-thinking, fine-motor, and problem-solving skills.

Group Size: Three or four children.

Materials: Small gardening tools such as trowels, bulb planters, small spades, and a watering can (if activity will be done outside, add small rakes, shovels, and hoes); and plastic flowers and vegetables.

GETTING READY

Introduce the topic of gardening by asking children to tell about their own experiences. Share an experience you have had or read a book, such as one listed below, with pictures of gardens and people gardening. Discuss what people do when they garden. Show the tools you have gathered, give children time to look at them, and ask children for their ideas on how to use them.

BEGIN

Add the gardening tools to the sand table indoors or the sandbox outdoors, and observe how children use them. When children have had a few days to experiment with the tools, suggest they make a pretend garden. Observe children, taking your cues from them. Extend the play at appropriate moments with questions and comments such as, "I see you're making long rows like the ones we read about," or "I think I saw some weeds growing near your plants. Which tool might be good for weeding?"

Children will probably come up with props on their own, such as using twigs for plants. But on another day, introduce the plastic flowers and vegetables. Ask, "What do plants need to help them grow?" Bring out the watering can and encourage kids to water their new garden. (The sand needs to be somewhat moist for the flowers to stand up in it.)

Help children anticipate "harvesting" their garden. For example, you might say, "I'd love some flowers for my table. When will your flowers be big enough to cut?" Some children might like to set up stands for selling the "home-grown" flowers and vegetables.

Remember

▪ Young threes may not be ready for complex interactive play. Have enough flowers and vegetables so children can each choose a few. Help them take turns using the tools, and, if possible,

provide duplicates of the tools.

▪ This is a period of great language and vocabulary growth. Children can acquire many new words in the context of play. As you converse with children, model new vocabulary to go along with their play theme.

BOOKS

Share these books about gardening with children.

▪ *Alligator's Garden* by Muntean and Rubel (Dial Books)

▪ *Grandma's House* by Elaine Moore (Lothrop, Lee & Shepard)

▪ *What Should I Put in the Hole That I Dig?* by Eleanor Thompson (Albert Whitman)

DRAMATIC PLAY

Have fun turning your setting into a cafeteria!

SERVICE WITH A SMILE!

Aim: Children will develop social studies concepts and dramatic-play and language skills while working together cooperatively.

Group Size: Four or five children.

Materials: Dramatic-play area furniture and accessories; a plastic or paper tablecloth; paper plates, napkins, small cups, and pitchers for pouring beverages; aprons; large sheets of white construction paper; a stapler; and tape.

In Advance: Create food-service hats for children to wear. To make the hats, place two five-by-twelve-inch strips of white paper together, and staple the short ends. Gently open up the strips and wear the crown as a cap.

GETTING READY

Gather together and begin a discussion about eating out. Ask children if they have been to a cafeteria. What do people do there? Listen to children's responses and build on their comments. Encourage children to compare a cafeteria setup to restaurants or salad bars with which they're familiar.

Show them the hats and aprons and talk about why workers wear them. Invite children to try them on and open a cafeteria where pretend meals or real snacks can be served.

BEGIN

Encourage interested children to set up a pretend cafeteria in a low-traffic area so that it can be used all week. If children seem to need your help, suggest they use large blocks to create the counter and tables where customers can eat, and kitchen equipment and food props from the dramatic-play area. (Be sure to let children design the cafeteria in their own way.)

When the cafeteria is set up, give children plenty of time to create their own play scenarios. Ask questions by assuming a role in their play. You might pretend to be a future customer and ask, "What do you serve at your cafeteria? When are you open? Where should I sit?" Let children tell you what to do.

Snacks...Cafeteria-Style

For a change of pace, serve snack in your "cafeteria." Invite interested children to be workers who set out snacks at the beginning of the cafeteria line or who pour milk or juice into paper cups at the end of the line. As children go through the line, "servers" behind the counter can give them their snack while "hosts" or "hostesses" can help them find a place to sit. Vary these roles at other snacktimes so that all children get to play the roles they'd like.

Remember

▪ Model good eating habits by serving nutritious snacks.

▪ Some children may not have much experience eating out. Pictures or a visit to a local cafeteria will help them understand much better.

BOOKS

Share these books about food and school.	▪ *Bread and Cheese* by David Lloyd (Random House)	▪ *Is This My Dinner?* by Irma Simonton Black (Albert Whitman)	▪ *No Peas for Nellie* by Chris Demarest (Macmillan)

ACTIVITY PLAN
READY-TO-USE TEACHING IDEAS FOR THREES

DRAMATIC PLAY

Everyone can find a role as part of a show!

CURTAIN UP!

Aim: Children will use dramatic-play, large-motor, and language skills.

Group Size: Four to six children.

Materials: Tumbling mats and other equipment for large-motor play, such as a climber, slide, balance beam, jumping board, walking plank, tunnel, and steps; hoops, ropes, and balls; and instruments and music.

GETTING READY

Gather together and ask if anyone has ever seen a play, a show, or any kind of performance, live or on television. Ask children to share what they remember. Ask, "What did the people do?" "What was your favorite part of the show?" Ask children if they would like to pretend to be part of a show.

BEGIN

Choose an area for interested children to play. (You might need to make room by moving a few pieces of furniture.) Let children know that you will help them move some of the equipment, such as the climber, into the area. Use other materials to add details they think the area needs, such as blocks to make seats for the audience.

Let small groups of four to six children take turns using the area. Some children may want to add props such as costumes to wear during their performances. To avoid tripping, safe choices are shorts, tights, tank tops, sneakers, and colorful ankle and wrist bands.

When interest wanes, officially "close" your show. You might gather everyone in the area to perform or to enjoy the show.

Remember

▪ To guard against "performing" accidents, you or an aide should supervise this area at all times.

▪ Mastering large-muscle skills is a favorite activity of threes, who also love an appreciative audience for their "tricks."

▪ Some children may not want to perform but will be content to be a member of the audience. Ask a child more than once if he or she would like a turn (in case peers' enthusiasm for performing is contagious), but let the child participate in her own way.

BOOKS

Share these books about performers and performances.

▪ *Ginger Jumps* by Lisa Campbell Ernst (Bradbury Press)

▪ *Chester the Worldly Pig* by Bill Peet (Houghton Mifflin)

▪ *Circus Baby* by Maud Petersham (Macmillan)

DRAMATIC PLAY

Use a favorite dramatic-play activity to encourage children to make new friends.

THE BIRTHDAY PARTY

Aim: Children will use dramatic-play, language, and social skills.

Group Size: Three or four children.

Materials: Dramatic-play household items such as dishes, pots, pans, toy food, play telephones, and kitchen furniture; and paper and crayons.

GETTING READY

At circle time, invite children to talk about birthday parties they have attended or would like to attend. Ask questions such as, "What is a birthday party? Who might have one? What makes a birthday party a special party?" Discuss the food, decorations, and activities that make birthday parties different from other parties.

BEGIN

Initiate the play with an announcement such as, "Today is Bunny Rabbit's (or Baby Doll's) birthday. Let's celebrate with a birthday party!"

Invite three or four children to set up birthday party props. (You'll want to repeat this activity several times during a week so that each child who wants to can help organize a party or attend as a "guest.")

Together talk about the items children will need. Stand back and observe as children go about their play — setting the table, choosing the guest of honor's favorite "foods," selecting dress-up clothes to wear to the party.

Let children develop the birthday-party activities in their own way. If you observe that the party is floundering, you might ask to be invited and encourage pretend play by modeling ways to interact: "Oh, look, Lydia needs some birthday cake. Tom, could you get her a piece?" As you observe and move in and out of children's play, be on the lookout for children who seem reluctant to join in and help them find comfortable roles to play.

Help to add new ideas and elements when you sense children have temporarily exhausted their own. You might ask how people know about parties and suggest children make "invitations" to send to guests or call guests on the toy telephone. (Make sure the guest list doesn't exceed the space in which children can gather comfortably.)

Remember

▪ Threes love to play birthday party, to talk about birthdays, and to sing the birthday song. Watch for birthday play to arise spontaneously, and then add the elements in this plan to develop concepts and vocabulary and to encourage expressive language.

▪ Threes are becoming aware of and fascinated by their own growth. Use birthday-party play to talk about how old they are, when their next birthday will be, and how old they'll be then. Discussing what they could do when they were younger compared with the things they can do now will help build self-confidence.

▪ If children become competitive or exclusive about who will be invited, defuse the issue by having them invite dolls and stuffed animals. Quietly make sure anyone who wants to has a turn at being a party host or hostess.

▪ If needed, enhance party play by inviting children to make party foods from modeling clay or to wrap up toys to give as presents.

BOOKS

| Add to the fun with some books about birthday parties. | ▪ *Happy Birthday, Dear Duck* by Eve Bunting (Clarion) | ▪ *The Surprise* by George Shannon (Greenwillow Books) | ▪ *Benny Bakes a Cake* by Eve Rice (Greenwillow Books) |

DRAMATIC PLAY

Gather your natural-born cleaners to spruce up their setting!

IT'S TIME FOR SPRING CLEANING!

Aim: Children will use dramatic-play, fine-motor, and language skills as they work together cooperatively.

Group Size: Three or four children.

Materials: Cleaning materials such as sponges, dry mops, feather dusters or dust cloths, small brooms or brushes, dustpans, dishcloths and dish towels, dishpans, and drainers; safe cleaning products such as soaps and detergents; and cleaning apparel such as aprons, smocks, and rubber gloves.

GETTING READY

At circle time, talk about cleaning. Ask children to share ways they help clean up at home. Show children some of the cleaning materials and attire. Help them name the items, and talk about how they are used or why they are worn when cleaning. Develop vocabulary by discussing actions people do when they clean, such as *scrub*, *sweep*, *dust*, *wash*, and *polish*.

BEGIN

Place cleaning materials in the dramatic-play area, and observe as children incorporate them in their play. Comment on what you see children doing: "You're working so hard to clean up your kitchen, Nicole." Ask questions to encourage discussion: "Daniel, you're such a careful duster! What do you like to dust?"

Add Some Soap and Water!

On a day when you have assistance, add water to children's play. Start with a small dishpan and fill it one-third full with warm, sudsy water. Place it on a towel to absorb the spills and splashes. Suggest that children who are interested wash dishes or doll clothes.

Clean the Whole Room!

Cleaning is often so popular that children will want to expand their cleaning play from the dramatic-play area to the entire room. Designate a special day — a warm spring one is ideal — to wash everything from manipulatives to furniture. While children are cleaning, lead them in this work song, sung to the tune of "Here We Go 'Round the Mulberry Bush":

> *This is the way we clean our room,*
> *Clean our room, clean our room.*
> *This is the way we clean our room*
> *And make it bright and shiny!*

Repeat the song, asking children to suggest specific tasks they are doing to substitute for *clean our room*.

Remember

- Threes enjoy cleaning, especially with water, but their dedication to the task at hand may vary. Keep the emphasis on play and fun, not on actually cleaning or completing a cleaning task.
- Cleaning with water and soap can be messy and slippery. Have plenty of mops and towels available, and supervise closely.
- Many household cleaning products are poisonous if ingested. Pay close attention and review safety rules about playing with or "sampling" such products.

BOOKS

Share these books with your young cleaners.

- *The Awful Mess* by Anne Rockwell (Parents Magazine Press)

- *The Big Tidy-Up* by Nora Smaridge (Golden Press)

- *My House* by Miriam Schlein (Albert Whitman)

DRAMATIC PLAY

Is the weather too bad to go outside? Plan a wonderful make-believe outing indoors!

AN INDOOR PICNIC AT THE BEACH

Aim: Children will use dramatic-play, creative-thinking, language, and social skills.
Group Size: Three or four children.
Materials: Props related to beach activities such as beach towels, sunglasses, hats, beach balls, and sand toys; picnic baskets; and dishes.

GETTING READY

This is a wonderful activity to suggest on days when the weather is lousy and spirits are low. If you think more children in your group have been on a picnic than to the beach, start your discussion by asking, "Who's been on a picnic? Where did you go? What did you eat?" Introduce the topic of going to the beach by reading one of the books listed below or by displaying pictures of beach scenes. Ask, "Have you ever been to a beach? What was it like? What did you do there?" If no one has firsthand experience, refer to the book and pictures and talk about what a beach looks like or what people do there.

Then present the beach props you've gathered. Together name each item and talk about how or what it is used for. This kind of exercise is wonderful for developing vocabulary and expressive language.

BEGIN

Put out the beach and picnic props and give children time to play. You may want to expand the setting of this activity by suggesting that children prepare a picnic meal at their "home," then "travel" to the "beach." If the play needs encouragement, ask questions such as, "What things do you need to pack for the beach? What foods do you want to eat at your picnic? How will you get to the beach?"

If children have made the block area their beach, you might bring over a large dishpan of sand for them to play in. Let the play develop in the way the children choose, commenting or asking questions as needed to spark new ideas.

Sing a Beach Song

Lead children in singing a song as they play on the beach. The tune is "Skip to My Lou":

> *Dig, dig, dig in the sand.*
> *Dig, dig, dig in the sand.*
> *Dig, dig, dig in the sand.*
> *Playing on the beach.*

Ask them to help add other verses such as *eating at the beach.*

Remember
▪ Add realism and spur science investigations by hiding beach treasures in the sandbox or pan, such as shells, driftwood, stones, and seed pods. Set an old shower curtain under the box or pan to ease cleanup. Then provide containers for sorting, magnifying glasses, and strainers with mesh of different sizes.
▪ Help spur threes' imaginations by pantomiming a walk on hot sand, getting into the water, swimming, etc.

BOOKS

| Share these books about the beach with children. | ▪ *Miffy at the Seashore* by Dick Bruna (Price, Stern, Sloan) | ▪ *The Paint Box Sea* by Doris Lund (McGraw-Hill) | ▪ *Titus Bear Goes to the Beach* by Renate Kozikowski (Harper & Row) |

DRAMATIC PLAY

Warm days make perfect occasions to take dramatic play outdoors.

COME TO OUR "CAR WASH"

Aim: Children will develop social studies and science concepts while using dramatic-play, language, and gross-motor skills.
Group Size: Three or four children.
Materials: Play trucks, wagons, and tricycles; buckets or dishpans; soap and clean water; large sponges, old towels, and clean rags; and chart paper and crayons.

GETTING READY

A wonderful introduction to this activity is a field trip to a car wash. If that's not possible, invite children to talk about times they may have helped wash a car at home or ridden through a car wash. Discuss the steps involved in washing a car, then list them together. Number the steps to help children recognize that there is a sequence to follow. For example: 1. Roll up the windows; 2. Go through the soap and wash area; 3. Go through the rinse area; 4. Go through the drying area; 5. Drive out to polish the car with rags; 6. Pay the cashier. (Let children come up with their own steps. They also might like to add their own illustrations.)

Now brainstorm a list of items you'll need to set up a car wash. Ask, "What can we use to wash off the soapy water? What will we need to dry off the toys? What else do we need to know to set up our car wash?" Invite children to create a car wash outdoors for cleaning the riding toys.

BEGIN

Together, choose a low-traffic area. Work with a small group of interested children to arrange the materials for washing, rinsing, and drying vehicles in assembly-line fashion. (You may want to post the chart nearby as a guide.) Give children plenty of time to play and develop their themes. If needed, you might want to encourage cooperation by inviting two children to work at each station and greet and take the money from customers, or suggest children trade jobs.

Remember

▪ Take pictures to use later to illustrate a group story about this fun event.
▪ This activity can be wet and messy. Hold it on a warm day and be sure children are dressed appropriately. You might request that families send along an extra change of clothing, just in case.

BOOKS

Share these books to inspire other outdoor dramatic-play themes.

▪ *A Very Special House* by Ruth Krauss (Harper & Row)

▪ *Building a House* by Byron Barton (Greenwillow Books)

▪ *The Something* by Natalie Babbie (Farrar, Straus & Giroux)

DRAMATIC PLAY

Challenge fours' creativity by pretending with boxes.

WHAT CAN WE DO WITH BOXES?

Aim: Children will use creative-thinking, problem-solving, and dramatic-play skills.

Group Size: Three or four children.

Materials: A variety of large, small, and oddly shaped boxes (including a large appliance box, if possible); art supplies such as glue, tape, scissors, markers, and crayons; paper plates; and odds and ends such as paper-towel tubes, spools, buttons, paper and cloth scraps, string, packing materials, and old knobs and dials.

In Advance: Ask families to donate boxes and assorted items. Observe children's spontaneous dramatic-play themes as they work with large blocks, unit or table blocks, and small props.

GETTING READY

Bring a few examples of the boxes and assorted items you have collected to circle time. Show children the large boxes and brainstorm together all the different things they could make, using them with blocks and riding toys. Children might suggest fire engines, washing machines, desks, computers, switchboards, airplane control panels, or ambulances. Then discuss how they might use the small boxes and other items to add detail and decoration. You might also share books like the ones listed below to give children additional ideas on things to do with boxes.

BEGIN

Leave the boxes and materials out, and observe as children decide what to make and determine other materials they will need. Let them pursue their own ideas, even if you suspect they will not work. Offer assistance if children ask for help in attaching an object to a box or seem ready to abandon play out of frustration. Otherwise, observe and let children use their own imaginations and problem-solving skills to create props from boxes. Give them plenty of time to experiment and to incorporate their creations into pretend play.

Build a Box City

At another time, bring in a collection of small boxes. Invite children to use these to create miniature cities. Also put out small dolls, animals, and vehicles in case children would like to incorporate them into their dramatic play. Later, encourage language development by asking children to dictate stories about their cities. Spark ideas with questions: "Where is your city? What's the name of your city? What kind of things happen there?"

Remember

▪ Some fours like to think a dramatic-play theme through before they begin. Let them approach the materials and develop their ideas at their own pace.

▪ If a child's first attempt at solving a problem fails, don't rush in with the solution. Instead, urge the child to try another idea: "That was a really good thing to try, Brian. What else could you use as headlights for your truck?"

BOOKS

Share these books about boxes to inspire builders.

▪ *The Box Book* by Cecilia Maloney (Western)

▪ *Boxes! Boxes!* by Leonard Fischer (Viking Penguin)

▪ *My Cat Likes to Hide in Boxes* by Eve Sutton (Scholastic)

DRAMATIC PLAY

Help fours feel comfortable and involved in "hospital" themes.

WE CAN BUILD A HOSPITAL

Aim: Children will use dramatic-play and social skills while working through emotions related to illnesses and hospitals.

Group Size: Four to six children.

Materials: Large blocks and plastic crates, blankets, large boxes, a steering wheel, empty plastic medicine bottles, stethoscopes, cloth scraps, and white shirts for uniforms.

In Advance: Collect books with pictures of people who work in hospitals and of the inside and outside of hospitals (see below).

GETTING READY

At circle time, ask, "Does anyone know someone who has been to the hospital? Has anyone ever been to the hospital? Why were you there? What did you see? How did you feel?" Then show children the pictures of hospitals and hospital workers, and talk about setting up your own hospital. Talk about the kinds of rooms they might set up, the props they will need, and what materials they want to use.

BEGIN

Invite a small group of interested children to begin work on the hospital. Suggest they use a part of the room where their hospital can be kept up for a while. Let them take the lead in deciding on the design. If needed, help them decide on roles to play and props they'll need.

Observe children's play and, as the hospital takes shape, move in and out with appropriate comments and questions. "Kim, I see you're a doctor. Would you like to measure your patient's height or weigh him?" Look for other kinds of materials which children could fashion into props. For example, you might set out a bathroom scale and a height chart or yardstick. Small boxes with pipe-cleaner antennas work as walkie-talkies. Provide pads of paper, pencils, and clipboards. Be sure to have an assortment of art and scrap materials so children can create other props they need.

The themes children choose, the roles they play, and the language they use will give you insights into their experiences with and feelings about sickness, health-care workers, and hospitals. Discussions at circle time can give children opportunities to share even more.

Remember

▪ A visit from a doctor, nurse, or other health-care worker can help to expand play. Make sure the visitor is comfortable talking with young children. Request that he or she bring along familiar items, like thermometers and stethoscopes, for fours to examine.

BOOKS

Share these books about hospitals and doctors.

▪ *My Doctor* by Harlow Rockwell (Macmillan)

▪ *What Happens When You Go to the Hospital?* by Arthur Shay (Reilly & Lee)

▪ *Your Turn, Doctor* by Deborah Robison (Dial Books)

DRAMATIC PLAY

Fours love to shop for clothes, so they'll love the chance to do it in your setting!

LET'S GO TO THE CLOTHING STORE

Aim: Children will use dramatic-play, social-interaction, language, and math skills.

Group Size: Four or five children.

Materials: Props related to a clothing store, including a full-length unbreakable mirror, a cash register, play money or materials for making play money, and paper shopping bags; clothing catalogs; various men's and women's clothing items, shoes, purses, and accessories; pads and paper for sales receipts; and sticky-back notes for price tags.

In Advance: Ask families to donate machine-washable clothing items for your store. Look through thrift and rummage sales for unusual items that will spark children's imaginations.

Launder all items before introducing to children. For health reasons, don't feature hats or any other items that cannot be thoroughly washed.

GETTING READY

Gather together and ask if anyone has ever been shopping for clothes. Ask children to share their experiences. Talk about how clothing is organized by type so people know what department or section to go to in a store. Discuss the people who work in a clothing store and the different jobs of each (owner or manager, salesperson, cashier, etc.).

BEGIN

Put the collection of clothes, accessories, and the cash register in your dramatic-play area. Then give children time to develop play themes. Some may want to play dress-up with the clothes. Others may already be thinking about creating a store. Observe their scenarios and, if play seems to need stimulation, you might take on a role and enter into the play by asking a few questions. For example, if children are playing "store," pretend you are a customer looking for a special outfit. Step out of the play as their ideas expand.

Set out art materials children might use to make props such as price tags and signs for different departments. Bring out other props you've collected, such as paper bags for taking home purchases and paper and markers for taking catalog orders.

Again, step in only if children seem to need a bit of inspiration. Then you might offer an idea, such as having a "sale," to expand their play.

Remember

▪ Encourage vocabulary development by modeling store-specific words — *customer*, *salesperson*, *cashier*, *price*, *sale*, *size* — in conversations with children.

▪ If children make props such as play money, rather than insisting that the bills or coins look like real money, let them decide on their own denominations.

▪ If possible, plan a field trip to a clothing store so that children can observe how the store is set up, how the items are sold, and what the different workers do.

BOOKS

Share these stories about clothing to help inspire storekeepers and shoppers.

▪ *Charlie Needs a Cloak* by Tomie dePaola (Scholastic)

▪ *I Once Knew a Man* by Franz Brandenberg (Macmillan)

▪ *My Clothes* by Diana James (Ray Rourke)

DRAMATIC PLAY

A spaceship in your dramatic-play area? How exciting!

THREE, TWO, ONE . . . BLAST OFF!

Aim: Children will use dramatic-play and creative-thinking skills, as well as their imaginations.

Group Size: Three or four children.

Materials: Interesting discards for making props, such as cardboard tubes for telescopes, binoculars, and microphones; old earphones, spools, knobs, and dials; and shirts and overalls for space suits.

In Advance: Look for a book about space travel to share with children. Two to consider are *A Day in Space* by Suzanne Lord (Scholastic) and *Magic Monsters Learn About Space* by Jane Beik Moncure (Children's Press). *A Day in Space* features clear illustrations about space travel, while *Magic Monsters Learn About Space* takes a lighter approach.

GETTING READY

Gather together and talk about outer space. Enhance the topic by reading a book together. Ask, "Would anyone ever want to travel in space? Where would you go? What would you travel in? What would you need?"

BEGIN

Gather a small group of interested children in the dramatic-play area and invite them to build a spaceship together. Ask, "How can we use chairs and other things here to make a spaceship? What else would we need to blast off into space?" Then provide children with the raw materials and let them take over. They may create control panels, space helmets, and other objects.

If you observe that children are stuck, ask questions to spur ideas: "Where will the astronauts sit in your spaceship? How will they talk to people on earth? What will they eat in space?"

Give children plenty of time to create. If interest is high, let this develop into a long-term project. The drama might even spill into other areas of the room, such as the block corner. There, children might create a "mission-control center" to guide the spacecraft or a planet for the astronauts to explore.

Sing a Space Song

Here's a song to sing with children as they blast off into space. The tune is "Farmer in the Dell."

We're blasting off to space.
We're blasting off to space.
Flying high away from Earth.
We're blasting off to space.

Invite children to add other verses that reflect the adventures they're having as astronauts.

Remember

▪ Space travel is an abstract concept for fours. Rather than trying to make sure that children understand it, encourage them to have fun with the theme. In other words, fours' space play will have more elements of fantasy then reality to it, so allow children to create their own scenarios.

BOOKS

Here are more books about space to share.

▪ *A Book of Astronauts for You* by Franklin Branley (Thomas Y. Crowell)

▪ *Let's Go to the Moon* by Janice Knudsen Wheat (National Geographic Society)

▪ *Watch the Stars Come Out* by Riki Levinson (Macmillan)

DRAMATIC PLAY

Children will love demonstrating how "big" they are by taking care of "babies."

A BABY NURSERY

Aim: Children will use dramatic-play, language, creative-thinking, and problem-solving skills.

Group Size: Three or four children.

Materials: A variety of baby dolls; baby-care items such as diapers and a diaper bag, bibs, towels, baby clothes, empty bottles of baby shampoo, powder, and wipes; baby furniture such as a crib, playpen, bassinet, and car seat; and baby bottles, plates, and utensils.

In Advance: Ask families to donate or lend any old baby-care items for a "nursery" in the dramatic-play area. Children love to show off things they used when they were babies, so encourage family members to let children bring in at least one object to share. If you are short on dolls, you might also request that children be allowed to bring a baby doll to school for a few days to care for in the nursery.

GETTING READY

A wonderful way to introduce the subject of babies is to invite a parent with a newborn to visit. Fours are fascinated by babies because they feel "big" compared with this swaddled bundle, yet may still remember being that little.

Ask children to share what they remember about being babies. If children have brought things from home they had as babies, ask them to show their items. Make a list of items that were probably used in caring for them. Discuss how each was used.

BEGIN

Collect the baby props and extra doll babies and place them in the dramatic-play area. Invite small groups to play. Some children may want to pretend to be a family with lots of children. Take your cues from them. A theme related to care may evolve naturally.

Give children plenty of time to let their ideas develop. If you feel they are getting stuck, join in the interaction by taking on a role. You might be a new mother asking, "Jeanine, my baby is crying, and I don't know what to do. What would you do?" You could also be a big sister and say, "My new sister is hungry. What do you think I should feed her?" As a rule, try to keep your involvement to a minimum.

Remember
▪ Build on fours' interest in their own growth. Ask them to bring in photos of themselves as babies. Post the photos at children's eye level. You might record their comments as they talk about their

own and others' pictures, and post these, too.
▪ Encourage language development by inviting fours to tell or dictate stories about their play experiences caring for babies. Children might also like to dictate and illustrate a booklet about "When I Was a Baby."

BOOKS

Share these books to inspire new ideas for play.

▪ *Babies* by Guo Fujikawa (Grosset & Dunlap)

▪ *The Baby* by John Burningham (Thomas Y. Crowell)

▪ *I'll Be the Horse if You'll Play With Me* by Martha Alexander (Dial Books)

DRAMATIC PLAY

Combine role-playing with fire safety for a great dramatic-play theme.

LET'S PLAY FIRE STATION

Aim: Children will develop dramatic-play and social skills while increasing their understanding of an important community helper, the firefighter.

Group Size: Four to six children.

Materials: Props for firehouse play, such as sleeping bags, telephones, large bells, fire hats and raincoats, plastic dishes and pretend food, and a rolled-up hose; a small step stool to use as a ladder; a toy riding wagon or long cardboard box to use as a fire truck; and an instant camera (optional).

GETTING READY

If possible, take a trip to the local fire station. Before the visit, talk about and record some of the things you might see. Write down questions children would like to ask. While you are there, take instant photos of the interior of the firehouse to post in your dramatic-play area later. Back in the room, review the list you made before the trip. Ask, "What were some of the things on our list that we saw? What else did we see?"

If you cannot arrange a trip, you might share *The Little Fire Engine* by Lois Lenski (Henry Z. Walck), or one of the books listed below.

BEGIN

Set out picture books and photographs of fire stations. If your local fire department is a volunteer one, the fire station may basically resemble a garage for storing equipment. You might discuss other kinds of firehouses and talk about how firefighters eat, sleep, and relax there. Let children decide what kind of fire station they want to create, even if you feel a more elaborate station would provide more opportunities for play. Children can always add to the setting as play develops.

If you notice that children are having difficulty planning, ask open-ended questions or take on a role in the play. You might be a firefighter and say, "I've been here all day and I'm getting hungry. Would anyone like to eat?" or "What can we do while we're waiting for the fire bell to ring?" Set out props for children to discover.

As children develop the theme, step back as they create their own dramas. This is a theme that may have appeal for many days, and children's play often becomes richer as they think of new scenarios and new prop ideas.

Remember

▪ Go over fire-safety rules and, as appropriate, subtly suggest children incorporate them into play.

▪ Encourage children to talk about their own experiences, and especially fears, related to fire. Some young fours may be confused about firefighters' actions, such as why they use axes and break things. Use books, videos, and talks to build understanding.

BOOKS

Share these books with fire-safety themes.

▪ *The Great Big Book of Real Fire Engines* by George Zaffo (Grosset & Dunlap)

▪ *Matches, Lighters, and Firecrackers Are Not Toys* by Dorothy Chlad (Children's Press)

▪ *Stay Safe, Play Safe* by Barbara Seuling (Western)

DRAMATIC PLAY

Turn your dramatic-play area into a pet shop!

CREATE A CLASS PET SHOP

Aim: Children will develop creative-thinking, problem-solving, and dramatic-play skills.

Group Size: Three or four children.

Materials: A variety of stuffed animals ; blocks, boxes, baskets, and milk crates for pet beds and homes; and props such as collars, leashes, dishes, brushes, and pet food.

In Advance: Be sure that all stuffed animals are laundered before using them for this activity.

GETTING READY

Invite children to talk about the pets they have at home, a relative or neighbor's pet, or pets they'd like to have. Encourage children to talk about how they or others care for pets. Ask, "What do you have to do to keep a pet happy and healthy?"

If possible, follow up this discussion with a trip to a local pet store. Point out the variety of animals, how they're housed, and how the people who work in the store care for the different animals. If such a trip isn't possible, read a book (see list below) and draw on children's own experiences with pet stores to discuss what they're like.

BEGIN

Set out materials you have gathered, such as the boxes and other items for pet homes, and invite a small group of interested children to play. Let children develop their own themes. You might suggest they use blocks to create tables and other supports for the pet homes, and a play cash register to create a place to pay for pets. Set out art materials — construction paper, crayons, glue, etc. — so children can create props such as signs or even make animals for the shop, such as fish or birds. Intervene as little as possible so ideas and scenarios come from the children.

Step back and observe the play. You might ask occasional open-ended questions, or briefly assume a role when you see chances to enrich a play theme.

Remember

▪ Encourage children to dictate stories and create pictures about the pet store or about pets at home.

▪ This experience can be a natural lead-in to getting a real pet for your group. Talk with children about pets they might like and decide on one that is appropriate. Discuss how to care for the pet and set up a special area together.

BOOKS

Use these books to inspire conversation about pets.

▪ *Pete's Pup, Katy's Kitty* by Syd Hoff (E.P. Dutton)

▪ *Pet Store* by Peter Spier (Doubleday)

▪ *What Do You Do With a Kangaroo?* by Mercer Mayer (Scholastic)

DRAMATIC PLAY

Fours will have fun acting out families' workplaces.

OFF TO WORK WE GO!

Aim: Children will enhance dramatic-play, creative-thinking, and language skills.

Group Size: One-to-one or small group.

Materials: Pictures of men and women working in nonstereotypical jobs in places such as a factory, an office, and a hospital; photos of children's family members at work (optional); magazines and newspapers in which children will find pictures of people at work (review for ethnic and racial balance); materials and tools used in the jobs shown in the pictures or that children's family members do; and scissors, tape, and crayons.

In Advance: Send a note home to families telling them about this new dramatic-play theme. Ask them to send in pictures of themselves at their workplaces, if possible, and any materials or tools from their professions that children may safely use in play.

GETTING READY

At circle time, ask children to talk about the kinds of work that their parents, older siblings, aunts, uncles, or other family members do. Encourage children to describe what family members wear to work, where they go, and any special tools they use. Ask, "Have you ever been to the place where your mother (brother, aunt, grandfather) works? What was it like?" If family members have sent photos of themselves at work, encourage children to share the pictures with the group.

BEGIN

Hang the pictures you've collected and pictures of family members at work in or near the dramatic-play area, at children's eye level. Add the props you've collected and ones families have donated to the area, and leave children to play with these materials in their own ways.

Create One Special Workplace

Pick up on children's enthusiasm and themes, and come together again to choose a workplace children would like to re-create. Brainstorm materials and props they will need to turn the area into that workplace. (If families have not already donated materials related to this profession, write a group letter to families involved in this line of work, requesting child-safe tools.) Introduce new props and watch the play develop and expand.

Remember

▪ Young fours who have never seen a family member's workplace may have a difficult time visualizing that person anywhere but at home, so don't expect everyone to provide vivid details.

BOOKS

Here are books with great pictures of people at work.

▪ *All About Things That People Do* by Melanie and Chris Rice (Doubleday)

▪ *Ho for a Hat* by William Jay Smith (Little, Brown)

▪ *Maybe a Band-Aid Will Help* by Anna Grossnickle Hines (E.P. Dutton)

DRAMATIC PLAY

Pretend play outdoors is just one more way to encourage children to use their imaginations.

LET'S CAMP OUT!

Aim: Children will use dramatic-play and social skills and have fun using their imaginations.

Group Size: Small or whole group.

Materials: One or two clean, old sheets; one or two washable blankets; rope; and various camping and picnic equipment such as sleeping bags, canteens and/or thermoses, picnic baskets, backpacks, cooking equipment, etc.

GETTING READY

Gather children together and ask if anyone has ever gone camping. You might say, "Where do people go when they camp?" "What are some of the things they take along?" "What do they sleep in?" Talk about what it might feel like to sleep outside, sit by a campfire, toast marshmallows, tell stories, and sing songs.

BEGIN

Share some of the props you have gathered. (You may need to add items according to what children have suggested.) On a day when the weather is nice, take the props outside and place them in an area where there is room to spread the sheets out. Give children plenty of time to explore and experiment with the materials, standing back and observing as they interact.

As you see scenarios begin to develop, enhance the play by temporarily stepping in to take an appropriate role. You might be another camper and say, "Hmmm, I'm sure getting hungry. Let's build a fire and make some lunch. Did anyone bring any food along?" Or perhaps it's nighttime and you are a camper who is a little bit afraid of the dark. You might say, "I'm a little scared to sleep in my tent alone. Is there anyone who would tell me a story?" Continue to allow the play to carry on as long as children seem interested.

Remember

▪ If children's enthusiasm remains high, find ways to continue the play outdoors the next day. You can store props in boxes, or, if the area is sheltered enough, you may be able to leave their structures out.

▪ Children may need your help "building" tents. Wait to see if they think of the idea and step in only if asked.

▪ As you take on a role, monitor your participation. When you feel that you've enhanced the scenario, step back out of the play so children can continue on their own.

▪ By taking on a role, you can help a child who seems reluctant. For instance, you might take on the role of a lost child who the reluctant child has found, thus entering the play as a team. Remain until he or she has been helped to find a role in the play.

BOOKS

Look for these books to share with your campers.

▪ *Lost Lake* by Allen Say (Houghton Mifflin)

▪ *Three Days on a River in a Red Canoe* by Vera Williams (Greenwillow Books)

▪ *How I Captured a Dinosaur* by Henry Schwartz (Orchard Watts)

DRAMATIC PLAY

Reach out and touch someone! Pretending to "phone home" can be fun and comforting!

TELEPHONE TALK

Aim: Children will use their imaginations and also practice fine-motor and math skills.

Group Size: One-to-one or a small group.

Materials: Several realistic telephones (rotary dial or touch-tone), a Rolodex or address book, and a unique sticker for each child.

GETTING READY

Display the telephones. Give children a few minutes to play and experiment with the phones as you help them identify the different parts such as the receiver, dial, and push buttons. As children play, ask open-ended questions: "Who uses the telephone at your house? Who do they talk to? Do you ever talk on the telephone? What do you talk about?" Then place the telephones in the dramatic-play area, and let children play with them in their own ways for a few days.

BEGIN

When you notice a child or a group of children using the telephones, introduce the Rolodex or address book. Offer to write down each child's name and phone number on a card or page. Invite each to choose a special sticker to put on his or her card or page, so that child can easily recognize her own telephone number. If a child is interested, encourage her to dial her telephone number by matching the numbers on the card with the numbers on the telephone. Children might enjoy pretending to call someone at home, then switching roles and pretending to be that person.

Remember

▪ This is a good activity to do at the beginning of the year. To help bridge the transition from home to school, try to arrange for family members to be available in case their child needs to call them during the day. For those whose employers discourage calls from family, request a schedule of break times and lunchtime when a call will be more permissible.

▪ When you notice a child who seems sad, approach her and ask about the problem. If it seems the child is missing a family member — and you know the person can take calls — suggest you call the adult to say "hi." Then go over to the phone together, dial, and let the child speak to the loved one for a few minutes.

Later, direct the child to the play phones, and enter into some pretend telephone talk with the loved one called earlier.

▪ Some fives will have difficulty matching numbers. Give them lots of time to experiment and practice without feeling pressure to get it "right."

BOOKS

Share these starting-school books with fives.

▪ *Sabrina* by Martha Alexander (Dial Books)

▪ *Shawn Goes to School* by Petronella Breinburg (Thomas Y. Crowell)

▪ *Willy Bear* by Mildred Kantrowitz (Four Winds Press)

DRAMATIC PLAY

Help children explore their feelings about the dark.

BUILD A NIGHTTIME TENT

Aim: Children will use dramatic-play and creative-thinking skills to create a night-like environment for play.
Group Size: Three or four children.
Materials: A table; flashlights; sheets or blankets; black, purple, and deep-blue construction paper; and aluminum foil, glue, white crayons, drawing paper, and tape.

GETTING READY

Invite children to name things they see in the sky at night. List responses and encourage them to suggest or add illustrations. If

children mention fears, encourage them to talk about what they are afraid of and what sounds or sights (such as scratching noises or shadows) tend to frighten them.

Share some pictures of the night sky, such as those in the books listed below. Talk about the moon and stars they see in the pictures. Then set out white crayons, aluminum foil, large sheets of black, deep-blue, or purple construction paper, and glue or tape. Invite children to use these materials to create a night sky. Some children will want to display their pictures or take them home. Others may be interested in using them in a dramatic-play activity.

BEGIN

Invite interested children to turn the dramatic-play area into a nighttime setting with the help of their nighttime pictures and a few sheets and other props. Show children how to tape their pictures onto the underside of a table. Then bring out the sheets or blankets and ask how they might use these to make a tent. Let children design the tent in their own way.

When the nighttime area is complete, encourage children to go inside with flashlights and explore the night sky they have created. Allow lots of time for play scenarios involving the tent and nighttime to develop.

Sing a Nighttime Song

While children are "star gazing," sing "Twinkle, Twinkle Little Star" or chant this old favorite:

> *Starlight, star bright,*
> *First star I see tonight.*
> *I wish I may,*
> *I wish I might,*
> *Have this wish I wish tonight.*

Remember

▪ Extend this experience into an investigation of nighttime activities. Begin with what people do at night. Include recreational activities and jobs. Later, read books and watch videos of animals that sleep during the day and come out at night. Find out what special adaptations, such as good eyesight, help them move about at night. Make a class book or create a group mural depicting all kinds of nighttime activities.

BOOKS

Share these books about the night.

▪ *Let's Try It Out, Light and Dark* by Seymour Simon (McGraw-Hill)

▪ *Light and Darkness* by Franklin M. Branley (Thomas Y. Crowell)

▪ *Night's Nice* by Ed Emberley (Doubleday)

DRAMATIC PLAY

Creating a library is a wonderful way to enhance children's love of books!

LET'S PLAY LIBRARY

Aim: Children will develop social studies concepts while using dramatic-play, language, and social skills.

Group Size: Three or four children.

Materials: Large blocks for building shelves and counters; a table for a librarian's desk; books from the room or children's homes; homemade books; paper and markers for signing out books; and signs or displays borrowed from a school or public library (optional).

GETTING READY

If your group doesn't go together to the library on a regular basis, plan a trip now. Take a tour so children can see how the books are arranged on the shelves and where to check out a book. You might arrange to have the librarian read a book aloud, then help each child choose a book to take home.

Back in the room, discuss the experience. Ask, "What are some of the things we saw at the library? What are some of the things that happen there? What would we need to create a library here?" Then invite children to brainstorm a list of furnishings and props. Together, decide the best place to put the library. Encourage children to share their ideas and give them time to plan on their own.

BEGIN

The next day, place some of the props on your list in the area you chose. Help children recall how books were arranged at the real library, and encourage them to think of ways to arrange books they gather from the room or home. For instance, you can provide paper strips and markers that children might decide to use for signing out books at the librarian's desk. Stand back and let the children create their own scenarios.

Remember

▪ Some children will be so inspired by the library, they'll want to make books to place in it. Staple sheets of paper into pre-made blank books. Encourage children to use drawings and inventive spelling to tell their stories. Be sure to give each story a title and have the author sign the cover. This is a wonderful way to encourage children to write and to introduce the parts of a book. "Librarians" may want to read their own stories during storyhour!

▪ Remind children to be careful with books. Together, make a list of library rules such as no scribbling on pages.

▪ This activity could last for weeks, even months. You may wish to start a borrowing system, so children can take books home overnight or over the weekend. Let family members know, and set up a sign-out system to keep track of the books.

BOOKS

Here are wordless books that are fun for young librarians to "read" aloud.

▪ *Bobo's Dream* by Martha Alexander (Dial Books)

▪ *The Snowman* by Raymond Briggs (Random House)

▪ *Who's Seen the Scissors?* by Fernando Krahn (E. P. Dutton)

DRAMATIC PLAY

Children love writing and receiving letters. A dramatic-play post office lets them do both!

WHAT'S IN THE MAIL?

Aim: Children will explore social studies concepts and use dramatic-play, social, and language skills.

Group Size: Three or four children.

Materials: Props such as old envelopes, junk mail, stickers, stamps and stamp pads, tape, and crayons; a large box for a central mailbox; individual mailboxes (see ideas below); and a large cloth bag for a mail carrier.

In Advance: Create individual mailboxes for play. You might give each child a sheet of paper to decorate, then, together, cover clean, large-sized juice cans. Help children label them with their name or special sign or sticker. Or give each child a whole paper plate and half of another. Together, staple the half plate

wrong-side-out onto the whole plate to create a pocket. Let children decorate and label.

GETTING READY

Bring in a few pieces of mail and ask children to do the same. Ask if anyone has ever gotten a letter or a magazine in the mail. Who brings the mail? How do you mail a letter to someone? If possible, plan a trip to a local post office. During the visit, talk about the workers' jobs and the other activities that are going on. Encourage children to comment on the physical setup, such as the counters where workers accept packages, the walls with mailboxes, and the places to buy stamps. If possible, walk with a mail carrier for a few stops.

Back in your setting, talk about what children saw. If a trip wasn't possible, share some of the books below.

BEGIN

Bring out the mailboxes children have already made. Set out construction paper and markers for creating signs and for decorating the big box to make a main mailbox. Then show children a few other post office props you've collected. Give children plenty of time to play and develop themes. You might be a customer and ask, "Where do I buy stamps? Where can I mail letters?" Let the play develop as children choose, even if it seems illogical to you. Take a role only to expand their ideas or help a reluctant child find a comfortable role in the play.

Remember

▪ To encourage lots of writing, set up an area with paper, markers, and envelopes. Make a list of children's first names and/or special signs or stickers to which you can refer. Allow and encourage inventive spelling. (The act of writing is more important than mechanics at this stage.)

▪ Get in the habit of sending group letters or cards to children and staff members who are ill or group thank-you notes to visitors or field-trip guides. Walk together to a nearby mailbox to mail the greetings.

▪ Ask family members to supply preaddressed envelopes with stamps so children can mail letters home.

▪ As a surprise, write and mail a letter to your group. Together, open and read it at circle time.

BOOKS

Share these books about the post office.

▪ *A Letter to Amy* by Ezra Jack Keats (Harper & Row)

▪ *I Write It* by Ruth Krauss (Harper & Row)

▪ *Letters From Calico Cat* by Donald Charles (Children's Press)

DRAMATIC PLAY

Fives have a natural fascination with caring for animals, so why not open a veterinarian's office?

THE VETERINARIAN IS IN!

Aim: Children will develop social studies and science concepts and use dramatic-play, creative-thinking, language, and social skills.

Group Size: Four or five children.

Materials: Cardboard boxes or blocks to use as cages; props for caring for patients, such as bandages, pet brushes and combs, and pet foods and dishes; and pads of paper and pencils.

In Advance: Send a note home requesting clean, old stuffed animals (as patients), boxes (for cages), pet dishes, pet grooming items, and anything else pet-related to use in the vet's office dramatic-play area.

GETTING READY

At circle time, ask if anyone has a pet, knows a pet, or would like to have a pet. Then talk about where people take their pets when they are sick. Encourage children to share their experiences by asking, "What are some of the ways a veterinarian helps animals? What kinds of animals does a veterinarian care for?" (You might explain that some vets care for dogs and cats, while others specialize in big animals like horses and cows. Zoos have special doctors to treat the animals there.)

If children are not familiar with veterinarians, you might arrange a trip to a nearby office, ask a friendly veterinarian to visit, or read a book about an animal doctor (see titles below).

BEGIN

Show small groups of children the props you have collected. Discuss each item and how it might be used in a veterinarian's office. Then set all the items out in your dramatic-play area. Give children time to play freely in the area. If needed, help them work together cooperatively to set up the office, letting them design it in any way they wish.

When they decide their office is open for business, you might suggest that they take the "sick" animals to see the doctor(s). Children will think of many scenarios on their own. If needed, you can help expand the play by "bringing in your own sick bird" and asking a "doctor" to examine it.

Remember
- Thoroughly clean all borrowed pet accessories before and after play.

- Ask family members to label donated items. Children can help make name tags for animals.
- Many fives love to plan their dramatic-play settings carefully. Allow time for them to work out details like location, construction of props, and arrangement of materials. Offer your assistance only as needed.
- Encourage language development by inviting doctors and pet owners to describe events in the office and to report on the "progress" of the patients.
- Children with little or no exposure to pets may have difficulty understanding what a veterinarian does. Assist their understanding by comparing a visit to a vet to a visit to their own doctor for a checkup or treatment.

BOOKS

Share these books about animals to spur ideas.

- *Animal Doctor* by Ezra Jack Keats (Thomas Y. Crowell)
- *Grabianski's Dogs* by Janusz Grabianski (Franklin Watts)
- *Too Many Rabbits* by Peggy Parish (Macmillan)

DRAMATIC PLAY

Fives will enjoy this new way to use outdoor riding toys on a warm sunny day.

CARS, TRIKES, AND TRAFFIC

Aim: Children will develop social studies concepts while using dramatic-play, creative-thinking, language, gross-motor, and social skills.

Group Size: Five to eight children (or more or less depending on the number of riding toys available).

Materials: Outdoor riding toys; costume props for traffic directors (such as orange vests), police officers (badges), and construction workers (hard hats); and art materials such as paper, crayons, markers, and chalk.

In Advance: If your program has only a limited number of riding toys, you might ask families to loan trikes, wagons, and other big toys for a few days. Be sure each borrowed toy is labeled with the child's name.

GETTING READY

Plan a walk around the neighborhood to observe traffic on the streets. Together, look for lines and signs on the roads. (Try to plan the timing and route so that children see road-construction workers and police officers or traffic directors at work.)

Back in your setting, talk about what children saw. Ask, "What kinds of signs did you see? What did they look like? How were they used?" Talk about the workers children saw. Ask, "Who did you see working on the roads? What important jobs do these people do?" Invite children to dictate a group experience story about the walk. Sketch signs children name and encourage them to use vocabulary related to the occupations they saw.

BEGIN

Propose the idea of playing roads and cars with riding toys outdoors. Ask, "What will we need to do this?" Help children who want to make road signs. Others may look through dress-up clothes for costumes or use art materials to create badges and hats.

Time to Go Outside!

When the weather is right, go outside so children can set up the "road scene." If necessary, suggest children decide where they want to put the roads, then help mark them with chalk. They will probably place their signs at different places along the road, decide who will be drivers, who will be road workers or traffic directors, and how to take turns. Only step in as needed and do so by asking open-ended questions and assuming a role. You might say something like, "Excuse me, Policewoman, but how do I get to

the shopping mall from here?" (If problems or disputes arise, give children time to try to come to agreements themselves before you step in.)

Remember

- Bring in traffic-safety rules as appropriate. For example, remind drivers to "buckle up" before driving off in their vehicles. As a fellow "pedestrian," talk about what children should do before crossing the road.
- Some children may want to set up a construction area in or near the sandbox. Wood and child-safe tools can add to the realism of the site.

BOOKS

| Share these books about vehicles and traffic. | • *The Bear's Bicycle* by Emilie McLeod (Little, Brown) | • *Have You Seen Roads?* by Joanne Oppenheim (Addison-Wesley) | • *When I Ride in a Car* by Dorothy Chlad (Children's Press) |

DRAMATIC PLAY

What's the special today? Have fun turning your dramatic-play area into a restaurant!

TODAY'S SPECIAL IS . . .

Aim: Children will explore social studies concepts while using dramatic-play, creative-thinking, language, and social skills.

Group Size: Four or five children.

Materials: Dramatic-play furniture and props, such as small tables, tablecloths, silverware, dishes, and aprons; note pads and markers for taking orders; menus from area restaurants; and large sheets of paper, old magazines with pictures of food, markers, and glue for making menus.

GETTING READY

Invite children to share experiences with eating in restaurants. Ask, "Has anyone ever been to a restaurant? How is eating at a restaurant different from eating at home? What do restaurants look like? What do you like to eat at a restaurant?" After you've talked, help children brainstorm a list of items found in restaurants.

BEGIN

Before children come in the next day, place the props mentioned above in your dramatic-play area. As children begin to incorporate them into their play, observe their scenarios. Later, pick up on and help expand their play by assuming a role. You might be a customer and ask what the special is, or apply for a job as a waiter. Keep your role brief. Then step back and let children continue to create, following their own ideas.

If children are interested in making menus, share some from local restaurants. You might point out how different courses or types of food are organized together. Provide large sheets of paper, old magazines, scissors, markers, and glue. Invite children to look through the magazines for pictures of food they'd like to serve in their restaurant. Don't expect the menus to be laid out in a conventional way.

As children play, you might casually discuss different roles to play — cook, server, customers, etc. — and the job of each. Decide on a name for the restaurant, and help children create a sign to display. As children get involved in the theme, you'll see many new ideas evolve. Again, suggest ideas only when you see play stagnating. For example, set out a cash register in case a cashier would like to "ring up" the checks.

Remember

▪ Consider offering children real foods to serve, such as fresh fruit and celery or carrot sticks.

▪ At circle time, you might discuss restaurant manners, such as sitting and talking quietly and saying "please" and "thank you" to the server.

▪ Try to arrange a visit to a restaurant at a non-busy hour. Help children decide on questions to ask the manager, servers, and cooks about their jobs.

BOOKS

Share these fun books about food.

▪ *Eating Out* by Helen Oxenbury (Dial Books)

▪ *Mr. Picklepaw's Popcorn* by Ruth Adams (Lothrop, Lee & Shepard)

▪ *Pancakes, Pancakes* by Eric Carle (Alfred A. Knopf)

DRAMATIC PLAY

Inspire millinery masterpieces with your very own hat shop.

HATS OFF TO YOU!

Aim: Children will use dramatic-play, creative-thinking, language, fine-motor, and social skills.

Group Size: Four to six children.

Materials: Assorted materials for making hats, such as newsprint, large paper plates, ribbon, yarn, buttons, bows, paper and fabric scraps, plastic packing pieces, markers, and glue; washable hats from the dress-up area; unbreakable mirrors; a cash register and play money; and pictures of hats worn by men, women, boys, and girls of different cultures.

SET THE STAGE

Set out the hat-making materials in the art area. Invite small groups of children to take turns creating hats. Children can use the paper plates or folded newsprint as a base, then add other

decorations to create their own unique designs. Help children, as needed, to make the basic shape of the newsprint hats or to attach ribbons to the paper plates to tie under the chin.

GETTING READY

Invite the group to gather wearing their new hats. Comment on each hat, then encourage children to talk about other favorite hats they wear at school or home. Discuss different workers who wear hats and why they wear them. Talk about why people wear hats for fun.

Show children the pictures you have gathered of people from different cultures wearing hats. Encourage them to point out similarities and differences in the hats they see. Point out details in the pictures that signal different climates. Talk about how hats can protect against cold wind or hot sun.

Now introduce the idea of a hat shop by drawing on children's experiences with shopping for hats. Ask, "Where can you go to buy hats? Have you ever been to a store that sells only hats? What kind of hat would you like to buy?" Allow plenty of time for children to share. Then ask, "How can we use our new hats to create a hat shop in the dramatic-play area? What else would we need? What roles can we play?" Record their suggestions for props and roles on chart paper.

BEGIN

Gather a small group of interested children in the dramatic-play area. Talk about how they can use the existing furnishings, such as the table, chairs, and dress-up hats as well as the hats they've made, to create a hat shop. Refer back to your chart and ask questions to expand their thinking: "Where will you display the hats to buy? Can customers try on hats? How will they know how they look in the hat? How will they know what a hat costs?"

Set out art materials for making props such as signs for the store or price tags. (You might provide more hat-making materials, too, in case children want to have a "made to order" department in their hat store.) Then give children plenty of time to develop their own scenarios.

Remember

▪ Some children will want to take their hats home and not use them for play. Try to have enough materials on hand so children can make hats for the shop as needed.

▪ Because cloth hats can spread lice, paper or plastic hats are much safer for play.

BOOKS

| Hats off to these new and old favorites. | ▪ *Caps for Sale* by Esphyr Slobodkina (Scholastic) | ▪ *The Hat Book* by Leonard Shortall (Western) | ▪ *Jennie's Hat* by Ezra Jack Keats (Harper & Row) |

DRAMATIC PLAY

Children enjoy a vacation almost as much as adults do! Build on their natural enthusiasm with this theme.

THE TRAVEL AGENCY

Aim: Children will develop social studies concepts as they use dramatic-play, language, and social skills.

Group Size: Three or four children.

Materials: Items gathered from a local travel agency, such as plane, train, bus, and boat schedules and posters of vacation spots; expired passports or broken cameras (borrowed from families); vacation clothing and suitcases; stamps and holepunches for marking tickets and passports; play money; and paper and markers.

In Advance: Contact a local travel agency and inquire about materials like those listed above that it might donate. Ask families to loan you expired passports or old cameras for play or to send in literature gathered during vacations which they no longer need.

GETTING READY

At circle time, invite children to share their traveling experiences. Also ask where children would like to go. Ask, "How did you (would you) get where you were going? Did you need a ticket to ride the bus (train, plane, boat)? What did the ticket look like? Who took the ticket?"

Talk about people who plan trips. Explain that a travel agent is a person who helps others plan trips. If possible, visit a nearby travel agency. If a visit is not possible, show children some of the materials you received from the travel agent. Explain how an agent would use the schedules to plan the timing of a trip. Show the posters and explain that these are places to go on vacation. Then place these items in your dramatic-play area.

BEGIN

After children have had a chance to use the props in their play, you might gather a small group and brainstorm how they can use part of the area to create a travel agency. (They may have already started themselves; if so, let them continue on their own.) If needed, you can suggest that a table become the agent's desk. Posters can be hung on the walls and literature displayed on shelves or block tables. Just remember, these are only suggestions. Be sure to let the children decide how to set up the area.

If roles haven't developed, you might talk about the different roles children could play. (Some could be travelers while others could be travel agents or transportation workers who stamp tickets.) Children may want to turn a separate room/area into a vacation spot. Then a traveler who buys a ticket from an agent can pack at "home," and travel to the destination.

Set out art materials so children can create other props they need. Observe, intervening only to assume an appropriate role that might expand play or encourage new roles.

Remember

▪ This is a good activity to do after a vacation break. Listen to children's experiences and build on them with this theme.

▪ Joining children's play can inspire new interest. Visit the travel agent yourself for vacation ideas. Be sure to let the children direct you in what to do.

▪ Some "travelers" may want to share real or pretend travel experiences through pictures or stories.

BOOKS

| Here are books about traveling to share with children. | ▪ *Airport* by Byron Barton (Thomas Y. Crowell) | ▪ *Davey Goes Places* by Lois Lenski (Walck) | ▪ *Thruway* by Anne and Harlow Rockwell (Macmillan) |

DRAMATIC PLAY

Fives will take off on wonderful adventures when they build their own airport!

AT THE AIRPORT

Aim: Children will develop social studies concepts and use dramatic-play, problem-solving, language, math, and social skills.
Group Size: Whole class divided into small groups.
Materials: Pictures of airports; suitcases and bags; a bath scale and wagon to weigh and transport luggage; ticket jackets, timetables, and baggage tags (ask a travel agent for these); other possible props such as toys for the gift shop; magazines, books, and newspapers for the newsstand; play food and dishes for the restaurant; dress-up clothes; art materials and recyclables for making props; and blocks and chairs for making waiting areas and airplane interiors.

SET THE STAGE

Add a few of the props listed to your dramatic-play area, such as suitcases and airline tickets. Observe children's spontaneous play using these items, noting their vocabulary and prior knowledge. Read or display books about airports (see list below) to enhance understanding and to encourage other play themes.

GETTING READY

When children have had time to play airport independently, gather the group and ask, "Has anyone ever been to an airport? What would you see if you went to one?" Share pictures of airports and continue to encourage children to share their own experiences. Talk about the jobs of different workers at the airport and on the airplanes. Brainstorm a list of places at airports such as a restaurant, newsstand, gift shop, etc. Together, select a site in your room for the airport where it can stay up for a while.

BEGIN

Provide children with the materials you've gathered, and observe as they work in small groups to create different areas of the airport, as well as props for play. Once the basic structures are in place, let small groups take turns playing in the area. Children can continue to add props and physical details.

Let children develop the play in their own way, while you look for "teachable moments" to elaborate on their ideas. Again, assume an appropriate role. You might be a lost passenger or a passenger who's lost a ticket or luggage. Or take a trip, asking children to guide you through their airport.

Remember

▪ A field trip to a real airport is a great way to spur ideas. If possible, plan one during the project.
▪ Fives are learning to plan ahead and enjoy long-term projects. Young fives may sustain interest in airport play for a week or two and older fives, even longer.
▪ Fives like to make and "read" their own signs by using pictures or by writing with inventive spelling. Some may also ask to dictate to you; others will want to print while you spell or to copy what you write.
▪ There are lots of roles to fill in this type of theme. Allow as many children to play airport at one time as you find can comfortably work together.

BOOKS

Share these books about airports with fives.

▪ *Airplanes* by Byron Barton (Thomas Y. Crowell)

▪ *Airport* by Byron Barton (Thomas Y. Crowell)

▪ *Snoopy's Facts & Fun Book About Planes* by Charles Schultz (Random House)

ACTIVITY PLAN INDEX: TWOS AND THREES

DEVELOPMENTAL AREAS AND SKILLS ENHANCED	ROLE-TAKING	SYMBOLIC PLAY	SOCIAL INTERACTION	COOPERATION/ SHARING	EXPRESSING EMOTIONS	CREATIVE THINKING	PROBLEM-SOLVING	ORAL LANGUAGE	WRITTEN LANGUAGE	SEQUENCING	MATH CONCEPTS	FINE-MOTOR
2'S ACTIVITY PLANS												
THIS IS MY DAY **PAGE 38**	■	■	■		■	■		■		■		■
FUN WITH PLAY CLAY! **PAGE 39**	■	■	■			■	■	■				■
WHO'S ON THE TELEPHONE? **PAGE 40**	■	■	■		■	■		■	■			■
TAKING CARE OF BABIES **PAGE 41**	■	■			■	■	■	■				■
BATHING BABY **PAGE 42**	■	■			■	■	■	■		■		■
GOING TO THE DOCTOR **PAGE 43**	■	■			■	■	■	■				■
WASHING THE DISHES **PAGE 44**	■					■		■		■		■
LAUNDRY DAY **PAGE 45**	■	■				■		■		■		■
LET'S GO FOR A DRIVE **PAGE 46**	■	■	■		■	■	■	■				■
THE SHOPPING TRIP **PAGE 47**	■	■	■			■	■	■			■	■
3'S ACTIVITY PLANS												
MORNING AT MY HOUSE **PAGE 48**	■	■	■		■	■		■	■	■		■
FAVORITE TOY VISITING DAY **PAGE 49**	■		■		■	■		■				
LET'S GO GROCERY SHOPPING! **PAGE 50**	■	■	■	■		■	■	■	■		■	■
GONE FISHING! **PAGE 51**	■	■	■			■	■					■
SANDBOX GARDENING **PAGE 52**	■	■				■	■	■		■		■
SERVICE WITH A SMILE! **PAGE 53**	■	■	■			■	■	■		■		■
CURTAIN UP! **PAGE 54**	■		■	■	■	■	■	■				
THE BIRTHDAY PARTY **PAGE 55**	■	■	■		■	■	■	■	■			■
IT'S TIME FOR SPRING CLEANING! **PAGE 56**	■	■		■				■		■		■
PICNIC AT THE BEACH **PAGE 57**												

ACTIVITY PLAN INDEX:
FOURS AND FIVES

DEVELOPMENTAL AREAS AND SKILLS ENHANCED	ROLE-TAKING	SYMBOLIC PLAY	SOCIAL INTERACTION	COOPERATION/ SHARING	EXPRESSING EMOTIONS	CREATIVE THINKING	PROBLEM-SOLVING	ORAL LANGUAGE	WRITTEN LANGUAGE	SEQUENCING	MATH CONCEPTS	FINE-MOTOR
4'S ACTIVITY PLANS												
COME TO OUR "CAR WASH" PAGE 58	■	■	■	■		■	■	■	■	■	■	
WHAT CAN WE DO WITH BOXES? PAGE 59	■	■		■		■	■	■				■
WE CAN BUILD A HOSPITAL PAGE 60	■	■	■	■	■	■	■	■	■			■
LET'S GO TO THE CLOTHING STORE PAGE 61	■	■	■	■		■	■	■	■	■		
THREE, TWO, ONE, ... BLAST OFF! PAGE 62	■	■	■	■		■	■	■				
A BABY NURSERY PAGE 63	■	■		■	■	■	■	■	■			■
LET'S PLAY FIRE STATION PAGE 64	■	■	■	■	■	■	■	■				
CREATE A CLASS PET SHOP PAGE 65	■	■				■	■	■	■		■	■
OFF TO WORK WE GO! PAGE 66	■	■	■	■	■	■	■	■				
LET'S CAMP OUT! PAGE 67	■	■	■	■		■	■	■		■		
5'S ACTIVITY PLANS												
TELEPHONE TALK PAGE 68	■	■			■	■		■	■		■	■
BUILD A NIGHTTIME TENT PAGE 69	■	■	■		■	■	■	■				■
LET'S PLAY LIBRARY PAGE 70	■	■	■	■		■	■	■	■			■
WHAT'S IN THE MAIL? PAGE 71	■	■	■	■		■	■	■	■	■	■	■
THE VETERINARIAN IS IN! PAGE 72	■	■	■	■	■	■	■	■	■			■
CARS, TRIKES, AND TRAFFIC PAGE 73	■	■	■	■		■	■	■	■			
TODAY'S SPECIAL IS... PAGE 74	■	■	■	■		■	■	■		■	■	
HATS OFF TO YOU! PAGE 75	■	■	■	■		■	■	■			■	■
THE TRAVEL AGENCY PAGE 76										■		
AT THE AIRPORT PAGE 77												

RESOURCES

Look for these materials to provide you with more ideas and a deeper understanding of how to help your children engage in rich and delightful dramatic play. The following books and articles can be found in a school or college library or bookstore. For information on the *Floor Time* video, call (800) 631-1586.

PROFESSIONAL BOOKS

■ *Children's Play and Learning* by Edgar Klugman and Sara Smilansky (Teachers College Press).

■ *Facilitating Play: A Medium for Promoting Cognitive, Socio-Emotional, and Academic Development in Young Children* by Sara Smilansky (Psychosocial and Educational Publications, Gaithersburg, MD).

■ *Just Pretending — Ways to Help Children Grow Through Imaginative Play* by Marilyn Segal and Don Adcock (Prentice-Hall).

■ *Looking at Children's Play — A Bridge Between Theory and Practice* by Patricia Monighan-Nourot, Barbara Scales, and Judith Van Hoorn (Teachers College Press).

■ *The Outside Play and Learning Book* by Karen Miller (Gryphon House).

■ *Your Child at Play: Birth to One Year; Your Child at Play: One to Two Years; Your Child at Play: Two to Three Years;* and *Your Child at Play: Three to Five Years* by Marilyn Segal, Ph.D. and Don Adcock, Ph.D. (New Market Press).

VIDEO

■ *Floor Time: Tuning In To Each Child,* a teacher-training program based on the work of Stanley Greenspan, M.D., for guiding children's emotional development (Scholastic Professional Development Video, 1989).

ARTICLES

■ "Achieving Knowledge About Self and Others Through Physical Object and Fantasy Play" by Judith A. Chafel, *Early Childhood Research Quarterly,* March 1987.

■ *Beginnings,* Spring 1984, special theme issue on make-believe play.

■ "Creative Play!" by Sandra Waite-Stupiansky, Scholastic *Pre-K Today,* October 1990.

■ "Dramatic Play: A Child's World" by Sandra Waite-Stupiansky, Scholastic *Pre-K Today,* October 1989.

■ "Encouraging Dramatic Play in Early Childhood" by Penelope Griffing, *Young Children,* January 1983.

■ "Facilitating Play Skills: Efficacy of a Staff Development Program" by Jean W. Gowen, *Early Childhood Research Quarterly,* March 1987.

■ "Increasing Preschool Effectiveness: Enhancing the Language Abilities of Three- and Four-Year-Old Children Through Planned Sociodramatic Play" by Ann K. Levy, Lyn Schaefer, and Pamela C. Phelps, *Early Childhood Research Quarterly,* June 1986.

■ "Social Pretend Play in Two-Year-Olds: Effects of Age of Partner" by Carollee Howes and JoAnn Farver, *Early Childhood Research Quarterly,* December 1987.

■ "Sociodramatic Play Training" by James F. Christie, *Young Children,* May 1982.

■ "Symbolic Play as a Curricular Tool for Early Literacy Development" by Carol Taylor Schraeder, *Early Childhood Research Quarterly,* March 1990.